KV-578-573

The United Kingdom and the World Monetary System

by
Brinley Davies
Head of Economics
Worthing Sixth Form College

Second edition

HEINEMANN EDUCATIONAL BOOKS
LONDON

Heinemann Educational Books Ltd
LONDON EDINBURGH MELBOURNE AUCKLAND TORONTO
HONG KONG SINGAPORE KUALA LUMPUR NEW DELHI
NAIROBI JOHANNESBURG LUSAKA IBADAN
KINGSTON

ISBN 0 435 84350 8

Published by Heinemann Educational Books Ltd
48 Charles Street, London W1X 8AH
Printed Offset Litho and bound in Great Britain by
Cox & Wyman Ltd, London, Fakenham and Reading

PREFACE

Most economics text books attempt to cover the subject within a single volume and in consequence some topics are treated briefly: often these same topics are those whose subject matter changes most rapidly. At present in order to keep up to date in the field of economics recourse must be made to a vast field of diffused literature including bank reviews, government publications, newspapers and various journals. With these problems in mind this series was conceived. The series consists of specialized books on those topics which are subject to frequent change or where the sources of information are too scattered to be readily available to the average student. It is intended that each book will be revised at frequent intervals in order to take account of new developments.

Derek Lee.

PREFACE TO THE SECOND EDITION

In this second edition it has been possible to update some information on recent events and particularly to devote more space to the effects of OPEC revenue on the world monetary system.

ACKNOWLEDGMENTS

The author and publishers are grateful to the following for permission to reproduce examination questions:
Associated Examining Board
University of Cambridge Local Examinations Syndicate
University of London School Examinations Department

CONTENTS

INTRODUCTION

Many economics students find the world monetary scene, and Britain's place in it, fascinating – but rather mysterious. This book is intended to present clearly, and at a reasonably simple level, the main ideas needed for understanding this topic. I hope that the element of mystery (but not the fascination) will thus be removed.

The first part of the book is theoretical. Chapters 1 and 2 examine the factors underlying the working of floating and fixed exchange rates, respectively. Chapter 3 explains the significance of the recent (post-1970) balance of payments presentation which Britain now uses. It shows too how the adoption of a floating exchange rate is reflected in the balance of payments presentation, including the total currency flow and the official financing section of the account.

The middle part of the book applies the theory of the first three chapters. It examines the experience of a rigidly fixed exchange rate system – the gold standard – up to its collapse in the 1930s (Chapter 4). It then looks at the International Monetary Fund system of managed fixed exchange rates, which came to an end in the early 1970s (Chapter 5). Next it examines the experience, since 1972, of floating exchange rates (Chapter 6).

The question may be asked: why examine, in particular, Britain's role in the world monetary system? The answer would be that Britain has often, for a variety of reasons, found itself in the very thick of international monetary activity. For example, the pound sterling was the linchpin of the gold standard – and when that linchpin weakened, and was finally removed (though this was not of course the only factor), the gold standard fell apart. Then, in the case of the International Monetary Fund, Britain was one of the architects and founder members of the new system; later, in times of balance of payments difficulty, Britain became on a number of occasions a beneficiary of the IMF arrangements. Again, it was Britain's decision unilaterally to float the pound, in June 1972, which ushered in the recent period of floating exchange rates – and which signalled the end, at least for the immediate future, of the IMF system. And then, as a background to all this, there has been the

1

continuing international role of the pound sterling as a major reserve currency.

The last part of the book deals with a number of proposals for reforming the world's money (Chapter 7); examines some more general aspects of the international role of money (Chapter 8); and concludes with four case studies, highlighting Britain's position in the world monetary system.

1
THE THEORY OF FLOATING EXCHANGE RATES

The foreign exchange market

In economics a market means a network of buyers and sellers dealing in a particular good or service. Some markets have a specific location (for example Covent Garden for vegetables). Other markets are not physically localized and are merely systems of communications between buyers and sellers. The foreign exchange market, which operates in foreign currencies, is of this type. London's foreign exchange market, which is the largest in the world, consists of over two hundred institutions. The most important of these are banks and foreign exchange brokers, operating by telephone within London and by telephone and telex with foreign financial centres.

The foreign exchange market is necessary because different countries use different currencies. For example, a British firm which imports cars from the United States will need to obtain dollars to pay for the cars, since the American supplier cannot use pounds to pay his wages and other costs, and even if he did accept payment in pounds, he would still himself need to turn them into dollars. Conversely a United States importer of a British product will need to buy pounds sterling to pay his British supplier. Similar considerations apply to the international buying and selling of services (invisible payments and receipts) and to international movements of capital. Often, importers and exporters buy and sell currency through their banks. Thus a British importer will probably use his British bank deposit to pay his United States supplier. The British bank will use its own New York branch to credit the necessary amount of dollars to the British importing firm, which can then transfer this money by cheque to its American supplier through the United States banking system. Meanwhile the British importer's deposit in his own bank in Britain will be reduced by the equivalent amount of pounds sterling.

Often, a bank will, in its currency dealings, be doing a similar amount of business in both directions; say, pounds-into-dollars and dollars-into-pounds. But if the British bank is, for example, on balance buying more dollars than it is selling, it will find its balance

3

in New York is rising. It will then have to sell dollars on its own behalf, and can do this through a foreign exchange broker, whose job it is to buy and sell foreign currency for clients, on a commission basis.

The market rate of exchange

Now that we have looked briefly at the structure of the foreign exchange market we must ask the question: what determines the price of a foreign currency (its rate of exchange) at any given time? The answer can be expressed in terms of supply and demand. We saw that exports from Britain generate a demand for pounds on the foreign exchange market. The lower the pound's exchange rate is, the more competitive British exports will be in terms of foreign currency. Here is an example. Suppose the London price of a Savile Row shooting jacket is £100. At an exchange rate of £1 = $3·60 it would sell in New York for $360. But at an exchange rate of say, £1 = $3·40, the jacket would sell in New York for $340. Thus the lower the exchange rate of pounds is, the more competitive are British goods overseas, the greater is the volume of British exports which are likely to be demanded and hence the greater the foreign demand for pounds. Conversely, a higher exchange rate for pounds

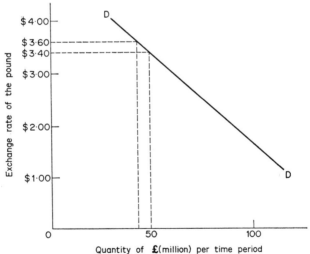

Figure 1.1

would make British exports less competitive, leading to a fall in the volume of exports, and thus also in the demand for pounds. We can thus draw a downward-sloping demand curve for pounds, which will describe the relationship between the price of sterling (its exchange rate) and the amount of sterling demanded by buyers of British exports (Fig. 1.1).

It is important to note that the elasticity of demand for British exports does not affect the direction of the sterling demand curve: even if the demand for British exports is highly inelastic, a reduced rate of exchange for sterling will produce *some* increase in export volume, and therefore in the demand for sterling.

Imports into Britain will generate a demand for foreign currency. Equally, we can say that British imports will generate on the foreign exchange market a supply of sterling, needed to purchase the foreign currency in demand. What will this supply curve of pounds look like? There are two possible cases.

The first case is where Britain's demand for imports is elastic. Here, a fall in the pound's exchange rate, say from $2.20 to $2.00, would, by making imports dearer and less competitive in terms of sterling, cause *the volume* of imports to decrease relatively sharply. So *the amount* of sterling being spent on imports, and thus supplied

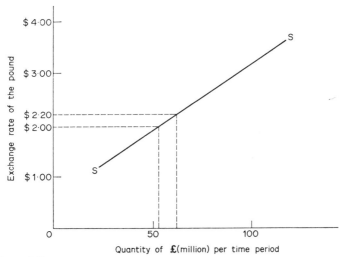

Figure 1.2

5

on the foreign exchange market, would also, to a greater or lesser extent, decline. Similarly, a rise in the sterling exchange rate, making imports more competitive, would lead to a relatively sharp rise in their volume, thus leading to a greater supply of pounds. So, if the home demand for imports is elastic, the supply curve of pounds will slope upwards from left to right (Fig. 1.2).

We may now see how the equilibrium rate of exchange of pounds would, for this example, be determined (Fig. 1.3).

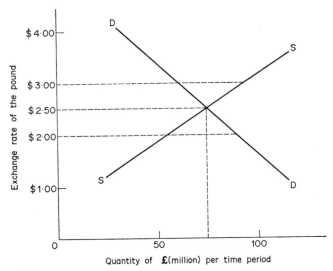

Figure 1.3

The equilibrium exchange rate would be £1 = $2.50. For suppose the market rate was only, say, £1 = $2.00. British exports would then be very cheap and highly demanded abroad, while imports would be dear and little in demand in Britain; so the demand for pounds needed to buy British exports, would exceed the supply of pounds needed to pay for British imports. This excess of demand over supply would, working through the dealings of the foreign exchange brokers, force up the exchange rate for pounds. *When the market exchange rate of a currency rises, we say it has appreciated.*

The reader will see that if the rate was above $2.50, the ex-

6

cess supply of pounds over demand would lead to a fall in the exchange rate. *When the market rate falls, we say the currency has depreciated.*

An inelastic demand for imports

Let us now turn to the second case, where the demand for imports is *inelastic*. Here, a fall in the pound's exchange rate, leading to dearer imports, would, by definition, cause only a small contraction in the volume of imports demanded. Therefore the value of imports, and the supply of pounds on the foreign exchange market, *would actually increase*. Similarly a higher exchange rate for pounds would decrease the import bill, and so also the supply of pounds on the foreign exchange market. Thus, if the demand for imports is inelastic *the supply curve for pounds will be backward-sloping.*

Is a stable equilibrium exchange rate possible in the case of an inelastic import demand? Let us look at Fig. 1.4.

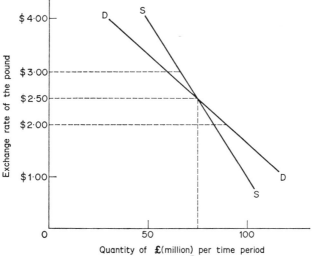

Figure 1.4

If the exchange rate is, say, $3.00 the supply of pounds will exceed the demand and the rate will depreciate. If the exchange rate is $2.00 the demand for pounds will exceed the supply and the rate will

7

appreciate. Thus there is, at $2.50, a stable equilibrium rate of exchange.

Consider, however, the following situation (Fig. 1.5).

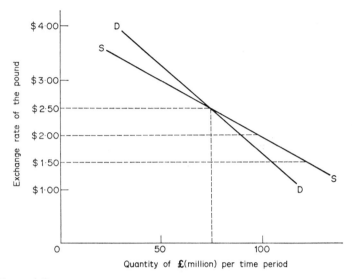

Figure 1.5

Here there is an equilibrium exchange rate at $2.50. But it is unstable. A reduction in the rate, for example to $2.00, would make the supply of pounds exceed the demand, causing a further depreciation in the rate towards $1.50, and so on. Similarly, a slight rise in the exchange rate would generate an increasing excess demand for pounds and the exchange rate would appreciate indefinitely.

It turns out, in fact, that the exchange rate will be stable provided that the *sum* of the elasticity of demand for imports plus the elasticity of demand for exports, is greater than unity. If their sum is less than one, the exchange rate will be unstable. This is called the Marshall-Lerner elasticity condition.[1]

---

[1] For further discussion of this rule, see, for example, J. C. Powicke, D. J. Iles and B. Davies, *Applied Economics*, Edward Arnold, 1972, p. 167.

How a floating exchange rate system works

In this type of exchange rate system the exchange rate of a currency is left broadly free to appreciate or depreciate continually in response to supply and demand pressures on the foreign exchange market – there is no official (fixed) rate of exchange. A number of countries, including Britain, used floating exchange rates in the 1930s, and again at various periods from 1971 (see Chapter 6).

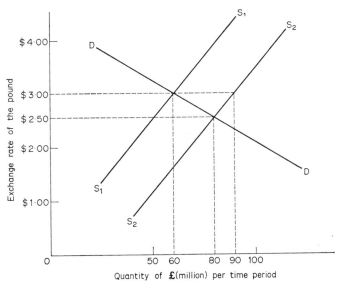

Figure 1.6

Fig. 1.6 represents a situation where the demands for imports and exports are both fairly elastic. In the initial situation, at an exchange rate of $3.00, the supply of pounds (that is, the sterling value of imports) is equal, at 60, to the demand for pounds (that is the sterling value of exports). In a simple sense there is therefore a payments balance. Suppose now that for some reason, say a tariff cut, imports (shown by supply S_2) increase from 60 to 90 causing a payments deficit of 30. The result of this increase in imports will be to make the pound depreciate to $2.50. This lower exchange rate makes foreign goods less competitive, and imports fall from 90 to 80. Exports, which are now more competitive, extend from 60 to 80.

9

Thus the depreciation of the exchange rate restores the balance of payments. Similarly an increase in exports, or a fall in imports, would lead to a new equilibrium situation, at a higher exchange rate.

Even if the demands for imports and exports are inelastic, a new equilibrium balance of payments is still possible, provided the sum of the elasticities is greater than one, as in Fig. 1.7.

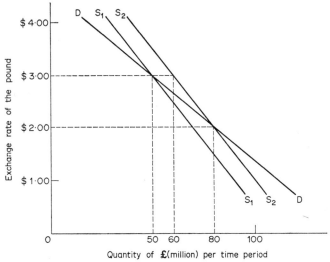

Figure 1.7

Here, imports are assumed to have increased initially by 10. Because of the inelastic demand for imports the lower exchange rate makes the value of import payments *rise* by a further 20! Against this, however, the depreciation of the exchange rate stimulates an extension of exports of 30. In spite of the inelastic import demand, therefore, balance of payments equilibrium is still restored, by the fall in the exchange rate.

It is clear that, provided the Marshall-Lerner elasticity condition is satisfied, a system of floating exchange rates could theoretically act as a useful adjustment mechanism for a country's balance of payments. How well such a system would actually work out in practice is another matter; this question is explored in the policy section of this book (Chapter 6).

The domestic price level and the rate of exchange

There are many possible factors which could cause a shift in the supply or demand of a country's currency on the foreign exchange market. One, which we have just noted, is a change in tariffs. Another, which is of great importance, is the price level of a country's goods, compared with that of other countries. Suppose a substantial rise in a country's prices takes place. This will make its goods less competitive, and so for any given exchange rate, its imports will tend to rise and its exports fall. In terms of Fig. 1.8, this would mean that on the foreign exchange market the supply of its currency would increase, from S_1 to S_2, and the demand decrease from D_1 to D_2. The net result would be a depreciation in the exchange rate from $3.00 to $2.00. Conversely, a fall in a country's internal price level, relative to other countries, would tend to cause an appreciation of its currency.

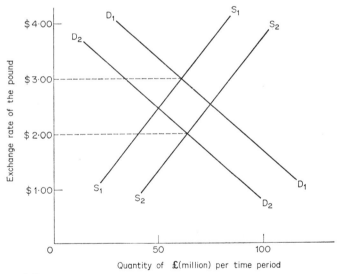

Figure 1.8

Sometimes this idea is expressed in terms of the so-called 'purchasing power parity theory'. This states that when countries' relative price levels change, the exchange rate of one currency against another

11

will settle at a level where the domestic buying power of the first currency in terms of goods and services is equal to that of the second currency. In its direct form this theory is clearly incorrect, as tourists buying foreign services often discover. When merely used in a generalized form it clearly loses most of its significance.

This point about the price level has an important implication for the usefulness of a floating rate as an adjustment mechanism for the balance of payments. We must now add an important qualification, namely, that the adjustment will be fully effective *at a given level of domestic prices* relative to other countries. For if a country is suffering from continual inflation, imports may be rising and exports falling so rapidly that a fluctuating exchange rate is powerless to achieve any lasting equilibrium. In addition, the rising price of imports, in terms of home currency, may lead to, or worsen, wage-cost inflation pressure, and generate a vicious spiral of rising prices and a worsening balance of payments. It would be a mistake to assume, then, that a country using a floating system of exchange rates may abandon a sound domestic policy. On the contrary, a harmony between domestic and balance of payments policies is very important indeed.

Arbitrage

Earlier we were looking at exchange rates mainly in a hypothetical two-currency context. In the real world, however, there are scores of different currencies and exchange rates. How are all these rates kept in line? This question leads us to an important activity of foreign exchange brokers, known as 'arbitrage'. Suppose, to take a hypothetical example, the direct pound-dollar rate is £1 = $2.00, and the direct pound-Danish crown rate is £1 = 10.00 kr. Then we should expect the 'cross-exchange rate' between dollars and crown to be $1 = 5.00 kr. But suppose, for some reason, the direct dollar-crown rate is in fact $1 = 4.00 kr. It will then pay a broker to carry out the following 'arbitrage' operation. First, he can use a capital of £100 to purchase 1000 kr. Next, he can use 1000 kr. to buy $250. Finally, he can use $250 to buy £125. So he quickly makes a profit of £25 on the operation.

As a result of the rush to buy crowns with pounds, the exchange rate of crowns against pounds will tend to appreciate; and for similar reasons, so will the rate of dollars against crowns, and the rate of pounds against dollars. In this way an orderly pattern of cross-exchange rates will quickly become established. The effect of arbitrage, then, is to smooth out exchange rates between different currencies. In arbitrage operations the broker is operating not as an agent for his customers but as a principal seeking profit on his own behalf (rather like a jobber on the stock exchange).

The forward exchange market: hedging

In the course of international business, importers, exporters and foreign investors find it useful to safeguard themselves against the effect of a possible change in the exchange rate of the currency in which they are dealing, by having available on promise for some time in the future, an amount of that currency at a specified 'forward' exchange rate.

Take the case of an American who has bought, as a three-month investment, £10,000-worth of British Treasury Bills, at an exchange rate of, say, £1 = $2.50. Suppose also, he thinks there is a risk that the pound may depreciate, which would put his investment at risk, when he later converts it back into dollars. It is possible for him to protect himself by carrying out a 'hedging' operation. In this example he could sell pounds to a broker for delivery in three months' time at the existing forward exchange rate of, say, £1 = $2.47. (Since the supply and demand pressures in the 'forward' market and in the present 'spot' market are not the same, so the two exchange rates may differ.) If, at the end of the three months, the pound has not in fact depreciated, his investment in sterling remains secure, and he merely makes a 'hedging' loss of three United States cents per pound, when he finally has to buy pounds 'spot' at $2.50 to fulfil the $2.47 'forward' contract he made three months earlier. If, on the other hand, the pound does depreciate, say to $2.10, he will make a foreign exchange loss on his sterling investment of $4,000, but against this he now makes a 'hedging' profit of $3,700 when he buys the now cheaper spot pounds at $2.10 with which to fulfil his original $2.47 forward contract.

Effectively therefore he has 'insured' himself against a sterling depreciation at a cost of three United States cents per pound sterling, to be set against the interest he has received on his Treasury Bill investment. The reader will find it useful to work out how an importer could 'hedge' against the risk of his home currency appreciating.

In a free-working market there will, for a given currency, generally be a whole spectrum of opinions about its likely future rate, shading from optimism into pessimism. The function of the foreign exchange brokers is to 'marry' the hedging operations stemming from these different opinions.

Summary
1. The exchange rate of a currency measures its price in terms of another currency.

2. A floating exchange rate is determined by the supply and demand for a currency on the foreign exchange market, as derived from imports, exports and other currency flows.

3. A floating exchange rate will tend to settle at a level where a currency's supply and demand on the foreign exchange market are equal (and where the country's foreign payments and receipts are therefore in balance), provided that the 'Marshall-Lerner condition' is satisfied.

4. The Marshall-Lerner condition states that a lower exchange rate will permit an improvement in a country's balance of payments, so long as the *sum* of the respective elasticities of demand for its imports and exports is more than unity.

5. Rapidly rising prices may undermine the 'equilibrating mechanism' referred to in paragraph three above.

6. Persons needing to use a foreign currency can safeguard themselves against possible future changes in its exchange rate, by means of 'hedging deals' on the 'forward' exchange market.

Appendix to Chapter 1
Capital movements and the rate of exchange
Foreign currencies are supplied and demanded for the purpose of investing and lending between countries. Let us take the case of long-term capital movements first. Suppose a British firm builds a papermill in Norway. It will need to purchase Norwegian currency to pay the contractors and workers in Norway. (In fact the position is rather as if Norwegian resources are being 'imported' by Britain.) Investment out of Britain therefore generates a supply of pounds on the foreign exchange market and will tend to make the pound depreciate. Investment moving into Britain generates a demand for sterling which, therefore, will tend to appreciate.

In the case of short-term capital movements the position is more complicated. Let us consider Fig. 1.6 for a moment (see page 9). At an exchange rate of $3.00 the supply of pounds (for imports) exceeds the demand for pounds (for exports). Yet the amount of pounds actually being bought and sold must be identical: a pound sold is a pound bought! The gap between the desired supply and demand of pounds will therefore represent an inflow of short-term capital into Britain – for the time being some people abroad are, so to speak, holding more pounds than they need.

One form which this residual demand may take is that the short-term trade debts of British importers for the time being exceed the credits of British exporters. (It is as if some pounds are temporarily 'nesting abroad' in foreign banks.) This could be due to a higher rate of interest in Britain: often, a balance of payments deficit is caused by domestic inflation, and a feature of inflation is generally a rising rate of interest, reflecting an excess of *ex ante* investment over saving. Also, the rate of interest may be deliberately increased by the government for the purpose of attracting a demand for pounds while the balance of payments is in process of adjustment. One vehicle for this might be a higher yield on British Treasury Bills.

This is a complicated area, and the conclusions above are highly simplified. One might however risk a generalization, namely, that most long-term capital movements are 'autonomous', and actively shape the level of exchange rates and the position of the balance of payments; while short-term capital movements, on the other hand, are sometimes (but not always) 'passive', being a result of changes in the basic trend of the balance of payments. At other times however short-term capital movements[1] may take the form of active 'hot money' movements, caused by the activities of speculators guessing about possible future changes in exchange rates.

---

[1] For a breakdown of types of capital flow see Powicke, Iles and Davies, *op. cit.*, p. 161.

2
THE THEORY OF FIXED EXCHANGE RATES

The technique of exchange equalization
Floating exchange rates were used by many countries in the early 1920s and in the 1930s, when, however, they got rather a bad name. One reason for this was that erratic exchange rate movements, sometimes exaggerated by the activities of speculators, caused uncertainties for importers and exporters. Another reason was the unscrupulous behaviour of some countries which unofficially depressed their 'floating' exchange rates, in order to boost artificially their exports and employment levels at the expense of other countries. After the Second World War it was therefore agreed to develop, through the International Monetary Fund agreements, a new and improved international system of 'fixed' exchange rates. In a fixed exchange rate system each country announces an 'official' fixed exchange rate in terms of a central 'pivot' currency, and its central bank then uses the technique of 'exchange equalization' to maintain this fixed rate. The IMF system operated from 1947 until 1971, but quickly disintegrated from then on.[1] A much more rigid type of fixed exchange rate system, called the gold standard,[2] had operated for a long period up to 1931. Fig. 2.1 shows the theory of the modern IMF type of fixed rate system.

Let us assume \$2.50 has been selected as a currency's official exchange rate ('parity'), this being a rate at which, over a period of time, it is expected the supply and demand of the currency, and the balance of payments, will be in equilibrium. Suppose there is now a temporary increase in the country's exports, increasing the demand for the home currency, pounds, from D_1 to D_2. The effect under a floating system would have been for the rate to rise towards \$3.00. Under a fixed exchange rate system, however, the country's central bank will 'peg' the rate at \$2.50. It can do this by supplying £25 millions, that is, purchasing that much foreign currency, on the foreign exchange market. In effect, it has then shifted the supply curve of home currency from point A to point B, in line with the original increase in its demand. Thus the fixed exchange rate of

[1] See Chapter 5.
[2] See Chapter 4.

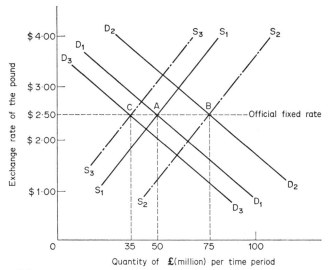

Figure 2.1

$2·50 is maintained. It will be seen that the central bank's reserves of foreign exchange will have risen by £25 millions. This technique of intervention by the central bank is called 'exchange equalization'; in the case of the Bank of England it is done through the Exchange Equalization Account.

Take the opposite case where a fall in exports takes place, thus putting downward pressure on the exchange rate. Figure 2.1 shows how the central bank can stabilize the rate by selling some of its reserves of foreign currency; that is, by purchasing pounds on the foreign exchange market. In effect, it has reduced the supply of pounds from point A to point C.

Under a fixed exchange rate system a country's foreign exchange reserves will therefore rise and fall according to the underlying balance of payments pressures. In the longer run, if a country's balance of payments is in equilibrium, the 'ups and downs' of imports and exports (and other currency flows) will tend over a period of time to cancel out, and so the average level of its foreign currency reserves will be steady.

The fixed exchange rate 'band'

It is not possible for a central bank to 'peg' the exchange rate exactly. To attempt this, it would have to intervene on the foreign exchange

17

market literally minute by minute, and in very exact amounts of currency. In practice, therefore, the market rate is pegged between fairly narrow limits, that is, within a 'band'. The central bank only needs to use the reserves when the market rate begins to approach the official 'ceiling' or 'floor' (Fig. 2.2). The wider the band is, the less a central bank will have to use the reserves to support a given fixed exchange rate.

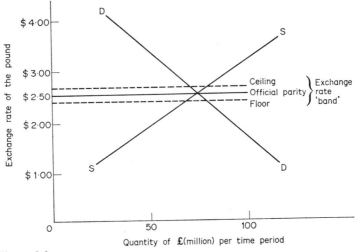

Figure 2.2

Under the IMF system member countries agreed on bands of, at most, one per cent either side of their parities. After the short-lived 'Smithsonian Agreement'[1] of December 1971, this figure was increased to $2\frac{1}{4}$ per cent, making a total band of $4\frac{1}{2}$ per cent for each currency. (The object of this was to make it possible for countries to use their reserves more economically.)

The role of the reserves
The reserves of a country thus play a vital role in any system of fixed exchange rates, for they act as a 'buffer' between changes in the demand and supply of its currency on the foreign exchange market. Without reserves it would be quite impossible to maintain a fixed rate. This leads us on to the next point.

---

[1] p. 55

In Fig. 2.1[1] the central bank was having to sell, when exports fell, £15 millions of reserves per period to peg the rate. Now if the central bank's total reserves of foreign exchange were worth say £30 millions, and if the import surplus continued, it would in a short time no longer be able to peg the rate and so a balance of payments 'crisis' would occur. Unless some other action was taken the currency would depreciate through the official 'floor' towards a new and lower equilibrium rate.

In the case of Britain, a critical position of this kind has several times developed, usually due to inflationary pressures. We saw above that a rise in a country's domestic price level tends to increase its import payments and reduce its exports receipts, thereby leading to an increase in the supply, and a fall in the demand, of its currency on the foreign exchange market. Under a floating system the currency would depreciate. Under a fixed exchange rate system however the pressure falls on the reserves. The more severe the inflationary pressure is, and the greater the gap between the demand and supply of the home currency on the foreign exchange market, the greater will be the reserves needed to support the fixed rate.

Dealing with a balance of payments crisis

Sometimes it is possible to prevent a balance of payments crisis developing. With sound domestic policies the government might be able quickly to reverse the inflationary situation, which would help to increase exports and reduce imports. If, however, a state of dangerously low reserves is finally reached, and if the government intends to continue using a fixed exchange rate, what can it do?

There are several possibilities. First, it could 'rig the market' by using exchange controls, import quotas, etc. to 'ration' the supply of pounds to potential importers. On general economic grounds, this would not be a satisfactory permanent solution (see page 85). Secondly, it could take measures to raise the rate of interest in the country so as to attract short-term foreign investment (for example in Treasury Bills) and generate an increased demand for pounds. Thirdly, it could borrow extra reserves of foreign currency, either from other central banks, or from the IMF.

These stop-gap measures might possibly do the trick. But if the balance of payments problem continued, the country might well have

---

[1] p. 17.

to take the final step and, with the approval of other countries, devalue its currency to a lower and more realistic fixed exchange rate. For example in Figure 2.1 it could choose a rate of £1 = \$2.25. When the official fixed rate of a currency is reduced we say it has been *devalued*.

If the demand for both exports and imports is elastic the lower exchange rate will tend to increase the value of exports and reduce the value of imports. If the respective demands are inelastic but their sum is greater than one, the lower rate will increase exports more than it increases imports. In either case the effect of the devaluation is to improve the balance of payments, in accordance with the Marshall-Lerner condition. If, however, the sum of the elasticities is less than one, devaluation would increase the gap between imports and exports and make the balance of payments position worse than ever.

If a country is suffering from the problem of an excessive balance of payments *surplus*, so that it is in danger of moving into a bad-creditor position, it may be necessary for it to *raise* its exchange rate. When this happens we say the currency has been *revalued* (or 'up-valued').

Conditions needed for a successful devaluation

We must be careful at this point. The Marshall-Lerner condition for the demand elasticities of imports and exports is a necessary condition[1] for a devaluation (or revaluation) to succeed in restoring the balance of payments. It does not however provide an automatic guarantee of an improved balance of payments, for there are several other important factors which must be considered. The first point, which is often overlooked, is that it is in practice often very difficult to estimate what the new exchange rate should be. Secondly, the country in question will probably need to reinforce its devaluation with a disinflationary domestic policy in order to maintain the improved competitiveness of its goods. Thirdly, it may need to take measures to free the extra resources needed for increased exporting and import substitution.[2] Fourthly, it should consult with other countries to ensure that they do not retaliate by cutting their own exchange rates.[3] The fifth point is a psychological one: the devalua-

---

[1] Except in one instance, see p. 23.

[2] p. 24.

[3] See Case Study 2, p. 98.

tion, and its supporting measures, will only succeed if they seem likely to succeed! We are referring here to the problem of speculation.

Suppose that a country's reserves are falling rapidly and it is believed that it may soon have to devalue its currency to a lower rate. People holding the currency will then have an incentive to sell it against a foreign currency, in the hope of buying back the home currency more cheaply later when it is devalued. If they have guessed correctly, they will make a good profit. If they guess wrongly, and the currency is not after all devalued, they can buy it back at no extra cost, apart from, possibly, interest charges on speculative borrowings, and any slight appreciation of the currency if it strengthens towards its fixed rate 'ceiling'. Thus if a currency is already weak, speculation may well increase the pressure on the central bank's reserves as it tries to defend the fixed rate. It was speculative pressure which delivered the *coup de grâce* to the pound in November 1967.[1]

The point also applies after a devaluation. If the lower exchange rate seems unlikely to succeed in restoring the competitiveness of the country's goods, a second one-way option, similar to the first, will present itself to would-be speculators, and further speculative 'hot money' pressures may descend on the currency in question, as they did on the pound sterling in the early part of 1968.[2]

Similar considerations would apply in the case of a country contemplating an upward revaluation of its currency.

Choosing the correct policy
Summing up, then, there are two basic balance of payments adjustment mechanisms which are open to a country operating a fixed exchange rate system. First, it can use disinflationary or reflationary policies to influence the level of its domestic prices relative to other countries. Secondly, it can change the level of its exchange rate. Which type of policy should a government use in a particular situation? The answer depends on the nature of the problem. First, let us examine the case of a country experiencing a short-term balance of payments deficit over say two or three years. Here the appropriate policy will probably be to disinflate the level of domestic income and employment, with the object of getting the country's price level back into line with that of its competitors. Under the IMF agreements a

---

[1] Case Study 2.
[2] Case Study 2.

country doing this was entitled to support its reserves, and exchange rate, by drawing on the IMF 'kitty' of foreign currencies.[1] When in due course its balance of payments position was restored it would repay its IMF drawings.

Second, there is the case of a country whose level of costs and prices has, over a long period, risen far out of line with those of other countries. It is therefore faced with such a large balance of payments deficit that years of severe deflation might be needed, probably at the cost of unemployment and slower economic growth, in order finally to restore the international competitiveness of its products. In this type of case, which the IMF called 'fundamental disequilibrium', it is better for the country, and its trading partners, if it uses the second type of policy and reduces its rate of exchange (combining this if necessary with disinflation).

Similar considerations apply to a country with either a short-term or a fundamental balance of payments surplus.

Summary

1. In a fixed exchange rate system, a country announces an official exchange rate, which it 'pegs' by means of the technique of 'exchange equalization'.

2. Exchange equalization means that a country's central bank uses its foreign exchange reserves to buy the home currency on the foreign exchange market, when necessary, to prevent it depreciating; and to sell it, when necessary, to prevent it appreciating.

3. In practice, exchange equalization is pursued within a fairly narrow exchange rate 'band'.

4. Taking the case of a deficit country, a balance of payments 'crisis' occurs when, as a result of a persistent deficit, the central bank's foreign exchange reserves fall to such a low level that the official exchange rate can no longer be successfully 'defended'.

5. Inflation may lead to a balance of payments deficit and, eventually, a crisis. Disinflationary policies, by restoring a country's competitiveness and reducing its demand for foreign goods and services therefore constitute an important balance of payments adjustment mechanism.

6. When a balance of payments crisis occurs, it may be necessary to seek balance of payments adjustment by devaluing the currency

---

[1] p. 41.

to a lower exchange rate so as to restore the competitiveness of the country's products.

7. The Marshall-Lerner rule is a necessary condition for a successful devaluation, but not an automatic guarantee: other important factors must be taken into account (page 20).

8. A country with a persistent balance of payments *surplus* may pursue a good creditor policy by means of *reflationary* policies or by *revaluing* its currency exchange rate *upwards*.

Appendix to Chapter 2
Supply elasticities and the rate of exchange

Supply considerations also influence the effect of a change in the exchange rate on the balance of payments. The factors which determine supply elasticities are many, and include the basic production elasticities (which tend to be high for manufactures and lower for primary products) as well as inelasticities due to artificial restrictions on payments and trade, such as exchange controls and import quotas. Let us take the case of exports first. If the exchange rate falls, no increase in export earnings (in terms of home currency) will result, no matter how elastic the foreign demand for a particular export is, unless additional export supply becomes available, either from increased output or by diversion of goods from the home market. Similar considerations apply in the case of import substitution. In other words, we were, for simplicity, in our early analysis implicitly assuming an infinitely elastic supply both of exports and imports.

However, suppose the supply elasticity of, say, Scotch whisky exports is less than unity. Then the extra export demand resulting from a lower exchange rate (whether under fixed or floating rates) will tend to increase the sterling price of Scotch whisky exports and part of their lower dollar price will, therefore, be eroded. Similarly, if the supply elasticity of imports is low, the foreign supplier may be prepared to cut his price to try to keep his market, with the result that the sterling price of British imports will not rise by the full amount of the fall in the exchange rate. So the improvement in the balance of payments would to this extent be 'blunted' by the factor of inelasticity of supply.

However, if in addition to the supply of exports being inelastic *the demand for exports is also inelastic* the opposite is true; a lower exchange rate then works *more effectively* in restoring the balance of payments! This is because the inelastic supply of exports will force up their sterling price, which will tend to increase export earnings. Similarly, on the import side, if the demand for imports is inelastic, it is best if the supply of imports from foreign firms is also inelastic, so that the price in foreign currency tends to fall, and the sterling price of imports rises, less than it otherwise would have done. So, even if the sum of the demand elasticities for imports and exports is less than unity, a reduced exchange rate might still possibly improve the balance of payments, provided the supply elasticities are low. In general, therefore, if demand elasticities are high, it is best for supply elasticities to be high; while if the demand elasticities are low, supply elasticities should also be low.

'Absorption effects' and the rate of exchange
Earlier we looked at the effect on the balance of payments of a reduced exchange rate mainly in terms of its price effect. However there are also income effects to be considered. In terms of Keynesian employment theory, a lower exchange rate helps to increase export 'injections' and reduce import 'withdrawals'; it will therefore tend to increase the level of income and employment in a country. The effect of this is to pull in more imports on to the home market. Also, a depreciation which increases one country's national income will (slightly) reduce incomes in other countries, and thus in turn the demand for its own exports. This means, therefore, that the effect of a lower exchange rate on the balance of payments will be weaker, taking into account both price and income effects, than it is in the case of price effect alone.

This can also be analysed in terms of 'absorption effects'. If a country has an import surplus, its total domestic consumption plus investment must be greater than its national output: its inhabitants must be using ('absorbing') more than they are producing. If, on the other hand, there is an export surplus, they are using less than they are producing – they are 'under-absorbing'. When the exchange rate falls in an under-employed economy, there is capacity available for the higher production and incomes generated by increased exports and import-substitution; consequently, there is no need for its residents' 'absorption' to decrease. The snag comes if there is already full employment. In this case real national income cannot rise in response to a lower exchange rate. Therefore it is necessary for domestic absorption to fall in order to make possible higher exports and lower imports. Probably it will be necessary for the government itself to bring about this cut-back in domestic consumption and investment,[1] that is absorption, by means of disinflationary monetary and fiscal policies – as we saw earlier when studying the requirements for a successful devaluation.

---

[1] As after the 1967 sterling devaluation: Case Study 2.

3
THE REVISED BALANCE OF PAYMENTS PRESENTATION

Since we have been continually referring to the balance of payments it is useful at this point to draw attention to the revised presentation which has been in use for Britain since 1970.

We can regard it as dividing into three sections.

1. *The current account*
This relates to the visible trade balance, the invisible balance and the current balance. Here is a summary of Britain's 1972 figures.

Current account	£ millions	
Visible exports	9135	
Visible imports	9827	
Trade balance		− 692
Invisible exports	5851	
Invisible imports	5141	
Balance of invisibles		+ 710
Current balance		+ 18

2. *Investment and other capital flows*
This deals with the various classes of long-term and short-term capital movements. Thus for 1972 we have the following summary.

Investment and other capital flows	£ millions	
Long-term capital	− 122	
Short-term capital	− 591	
Total capital flows		− 713
Balancing item		− 570
Total		− 1283

We find that £1283 millions of capital left Britain in 1972. It is important to note that the 'balancing items' refers to the statistical errors and omissions which any such table is bound to contain (*it has nothing to do with changes in the foreign exchange reserves*).

If we add the balance on current account to the balance of invest-

26

ment and other capital flows, we obtain the *total currency flow*. Thus for Britain in 1972:

	£ millions
Current balance	+ 18
Total capital flows (including balancing item)	— 1283
Total currency flow	— 1265

Two other items included in this section of the balance of payments were: allocations of Special Drawing Rights ('paper gold') to Britain from the International Monetary Fund; and subscription of (real) gold by Britain to the IMF.

Our summary of the balance of payments for 1972 now becomes:

	£ millions	
Current balance	+ 18	
All capital flows	— 1283	
Total currency flow		— 1265
Allocation of SDRs		+ 124
Gold subscription to IMF		nil
Total		— 1141

These first two sections of the new balance of payments presentation record, as it were, the basic fact of life of a country's payments position with the rest of the world. If, over a period of time, the total currency flow is zero then the country in question is just paying its way with other countries. If the total currency flow is negative then the country in question has a payments deficit which sooner or later it will have to deal with. If the total currency flow is positive over a period of years the country may be moving towards a bad creditor position. In the short run, of course, fluctuations in the total currency flow are to be expected, in line with temporary pressures, such as seasonal trade factors, or short-term capital movements.

3. *Official financing*

This section records how the total currency flow (together with the SDR/gold position) has been financed. Thus in 1972 Britain needed to 'find' £1141 millions.

Official financing	*£ millions*
Repayment of IMF drawings	− 415
Borrowings from foreign central banks	+ 864
Drawings on foreign exchange reserves	+ 692
Total official financing	+ 1141

If we look at the balance of payments for 1968, which was a weak year, we find the total currency flow was minus £1410 millions. This reflected, first, a weak current balance (minus £319 millions), and secondly, a weak capital flows situation (minus £1091 millions), which in turn was largely due to nervous 'hot money' sales of pounds on the foreign exchange market. In 1968, Britain's reserves fell by £114 millions; and the Bank of England had to borrow abroad to the extent of £1296 millions, to finance the remainder of the total currency flow.

Floating exchange rates and the balance of payments presentation
The logic of the new balance of payments format is, in principle, the same whatever system of exchange rates Britain is using. With a floating exchange rate however the role of the official financing section diminishes. In theory, if there was an absolutely free rate, there would be no need for the Bank of England to use, or hold, foreign exchange reserves; or to exchange credits with other central banks; or to use the currency pool at the IMF. The burden of financing any payments disequilibrium would therefore fall exclusively on short-term capital movements. In this case the total currency flow would automatically be zero and it would cease to be a useful concept. One possible indicator of a payments imbalance would have to be the trend of the exchange rate; another would be the current account balance plus estimates of the balance of independent long-term capital flows.[1] In practice, however, central banks using a floating exchange rate often carry out minor currency operations on the market to 'smooth out' the more extreme fluctuations in the rate. To this extent changes in the reserves, central bank credits, and even possibly IMF drawings, would continue (on a smaller scale) to be used, and recorded in the official financing account.

---

[1] Formerly called the 'basic balance'.

The 1973 balance of payments figures: a comment

The figures are presented below in order partly that the reader may better understand Britain's 1973 balance of payments position.

	£ millions	
Visible trade	− 2344	
Invisibles	+ 903	
Current balance		− 1441
Public sector borrowing	+ 829	
Other capital flows	+ 418	
Balancing item	+ 402	
Total capital		+ 1649
Total currency flow		+ 208
Net official borrowing		nil
Fall in reserves		− 208

The figures however contain a possible pitfall for the reader. It will be seen that there was a *net currency inflow* in 1973 of £208 millions, which, in the official financing section, was added to Britain's foreign exchange reserves. The reader might therefore deduce that Britain was 'paying its way' in the world in 1973 – in spite of its massive current account deficit of £1441 millions!

What actually happened was this. A considerable part of this deficit was financed through huge borrowings (£829 millions) by Britain's public sector (mainly the nationalized industries) on foreign capital markets – in particular the Euro-currency markets.[1] However, as the table shows, *such borrowings are not included in the official financing section of the balance of payments* (where logically they really belong) but instead in the capital flows section. In other words Britain certainly had, in a fundamental sense, a large payments deficit in 1973: but it was financed to a considerable extent on an unofficial basis, through 'ghost' borrowings abroad by Britain's government sector. Hence the rather misleading impression given by the 'bogus' positive total currency flow of £208 millions.

[1] See p. 110.

4
THE EXPERIENCE OF THE GOLD STANDARD

The swing of the pendulum
In the previous sections we looked at the theory of the two basic types of exchange rate system, namely, fixed exchange rates and floating exchange rates. We shall now examine how these systems have worked out in practice, in relation to the particular circumstances and the economic policies of the country operating them. If we look back through time we find there has been a continual 'swing of the pendulum' in the type of system in use.

Thus if we examine the systems chosen by Britain for the pound, we find the following pattern (in peace time).

TABLE 4.1   BRITAIN'S CHOICE OF EXCHANGE RATE SYSTEMS

Gold standard	IMF system	Floating exchange rate
1821 to 1914		
		1918 to 1925
1925 to 1931		
		1931 to 1939
	1947 to Aug. 1971	
		Aug. 1971 to Dec. 1971
	Dec. 1971 to June 1972	
		June 1972 —

It might be inferred, therefore, that neither floating exchange rates nor fixed exchange rates have a monopoly of advantages or disadvantages. One might even hazard that the wisdom and skill with which countries operate an exchange rate system may be as important as the type which they choose!

In this chapter we shall look at the working of the gold standard. There are two good reasons for doing this. First, it provides an insight into the practical difficulties of operating a very rigid fixed exchange rate system. Secondly, it will help us later in the book to judge the merits of certain proposals which have recently been made for a return to the gold standard, as an answer to international monetary problems in the early 1970s.

The theoretical working of the gold standard

Unlike the IMF adjustable peg system, in which the fixed exchange rate of a national currency was allowed, when appropriate, to be devalued or revalued from time to time, *the gold standard was a system of rigidly fixed exchange rates.* It was based on two principles. First, holders of paper currency issued by a central bank, such as the Bank of England, were allowed to exchange it for gold coin or gold bullion at a given rate (for example, one ounce of gold in 1914 was worth about £3·85). This meant that exchange rates between different currencies would therefore be fixed. The second principle was that gold could be shipped in and out of countries to finance foreign trade.

The gold standard worked theoretically like this. Suppose for some reason a country's imports increased, so that it moved into a deficit on its balance of payments. More gold would then leave the country to pay for imports, than would enter it as receipts from exports. Consequently the stock of money in the country, in the form of circulating gold coins (together with paper money and bank deposits backed directly or indirectly by the central bank's reserves of gold), would decrease. The reduction in the money supply would lead to a corresponding reduction in prices, which would begin to restore the competitiveness of the country's products, thus leading to a recovery in its balance of payments. The process of adjustment would continue until its payments deficit, and the gold outflow, in due course ceased. Conversely, a country gaining gold from a payments surplus would experience a reflation of prices which would restore its balance of payments, whereupon the gold inflow would cease. The gold standard

TABLE 4.2   THEORETICAL WORKING OF THE GOLD STANDARD

Stage	Country A	Country B
1	Balance of payments deficit	Balance of payments surplus
2	Gold is shipped to B	Gold is shipped from A
3	Money supply contracts	Money supply expands
4	Prices fall	Prices rise
5	Imports decrease; exports increase	Imports increase; exports decrease
6	Gold flow ceases: equilibrium restored	Gold flow ceases: equilibrium restored

31

was therefore held to provide an automatic balance of payments adjustment mechanism.

The amount of gold which needed to be shipped between countries in the days of the gold standard was actually quite small. There were thought to be two explanations for this. First (taking the case of a deficit country), a disinflationary situation would tend to lead to higher interest rates, which would attract short-term capital into the country and so reduce the rate of gold outflow necessary. In the period up to 1914, foreign investors were generally confident about the future stability of exchange rates and national price levels, and so quite small changes in interest rates would lead to substantial short-term 'balancing' capital flows. (This effect was reinforced by the international use of the pound sterling, which was 'as good as gold', and which could be conveniently transferred internationally by telegraph).

A second explanation for the low level of gold movements was the fact that in most countries gold was the base for a large pyramid of bank- and paper-money. This meant that quite small gold flows would lead to large changes in the total domestic money supply, and so to a more effective balance of payments adjustment.

The gold standard was argued to have two important advantages. First, gold flows between countries would tend to equalize their relative price levels and this would encourage international trade and investment and foster the world's economic development.[1] Secondly, the system was believed to function 'automatically' not just in the sense that international gold movements would provide a self-acting balance of payments adjustment mechanism, but also in the sense that it would impose a compelling discipline on countries to avoid unsound policies.

Drawbacks of the gold standard: 1. the unemployment risk
Unfortunately, the gold standard had drawbacks and these became so serious that, in the end, it collapsed and was never fully restored. The first drawback can be examined in terms of the 'Equation of Exchange'. This states that $MV = PT$; where M is a country's stock of money, V is the velocity of circulation of this money stock, P measures the price level in the country, and T measures the volume of output sold in that country. (For example, in a hypothetical community, 100 units of money, M, circulating 10 times, V, could buy 20 units of output T, sold at a price of 50 each, P.) In the case of a

---

[1] See Chapter 8.

country losing gold through a balance of payments deficit a fall in the money supply, M, was supposed to be directly reflected in a lower price level, P, leaving the level of its output, T, unchanged.

In fact however prices and costs in manufacturing countries tend to be sticky, particularly in a downward direction (the ratchet effect). This is due partly to monopolistic tendencies among firms and trade unions. So a fall in M in a country losing gold through a balance of payments deficit, was likely to be reflected not just in a fall in P, but also in reduced output and employment, T. *Now this fall in employment (and incomes) would of itself reduce the country's demand for imports and so help to improve its balance of payments.* Conversely, a surplus country gaining gold would tend, at least to some extent, to experience an increase in real income, leading to a higher demand for imports, and a reduced payments surplus. In other words, the gold standard would be 'working' for the wrong reason.

Modern macro-economics shows that a change in imports or exports has a *direct* effect on the national income, which is quite distinct from any income and employment changes occurring due to changes in the gold or money supply. In Keynesian employment theory, exports are regarded as a direct injection of spending into, and imports as a withdrawal from, the domestic circulation of incomes and production. Thus a fall in exports reduces, through a multiplier effect, the level of a country's income and employment. Conversely, a rise in exports causes an increase in incomes and employment leading to a rise in imports. The amplitude of these changes in income and employment, working through the 'export' multiplier, will depend on a country's marginal propensity to import.

All this adds up to a very serious case against the effectiveness of the gold standard mechanism, for it shows that balance of payments adjustments between countries might take place partly, or even mainly, at the expense of deflationary unemployment, in the case of a deficit country and, possibly, inflation in the case of a surplus country. In the heyday of the gold standard fluctuations in employment were of course noticed – but they were more often than not put down to other factors, such as the effects of sudden changes in gold supplies arising from new gold mining discoveries, rather than to intrinsic defects in the gold standard mechanism.

Britain's unemployment problem in the 1920s

Before 1914, the exchange rate of the pound in terms of the dollar was $4.86 (one pound being convertible into 0·257 ounces of gold, and one dollar into 0·053 ounces). During the First World War, when the convertibility of the pound into gold was suspended, inflation led to a substantial increase in Britain's costs and prices. So after the War, when the British government took the decision to return, in due course, to the gold standard, it was necessary to choose between two methods of restoring the competitiveness of British goods. The first was to select a lower exchange rate for the pound. The other was to adopt the old $4.86 rate of exchange and to back it up with deflationary measures aimed at bringing Britain's costs and prices down in line with those of its competitors. In the end, the British government chose the second alternative, partly with the object of making it clear that the pound would continue to be a key international currency, and that London would remain a major international financial centre.

The attempt to deflate British costs and prices was to prove a long struggle, and it led to heavy unemployment, particularly since the trade unions (not unnaturally) resisted the cuts in money wages required by the theory of the gold standard. Early in 1920 the exchange rate of the (now floating) pound was $3.40, and although it rose to $4.70 in 1923, it later depreciated to $4.40 in 1924. However, in 1925, when a policy of high interest rates had attracted foreign short-term capital into Britain, the Chancellor of the Exchequer (Winston Churchill) was able to announce Britain's return to the gold standard at the pre-1914 exchange rate of sterling.

Unfortunately, the pound proved to be over-valued at $4.86: at this exchange rate British goods were not fully competitive with foreign products. And so the balance of payments remained weak. Moreover there was little help for Britain from rising prices in countries with a balance of payments surplus; for example United States costs and prices remained stable in spite of the economic boom in that country. So it was necessary for several more years, for Britain to struggle on with deflation to underpin its balance of payments. (Later, Churchill was to refer to his decision to adopt in 1925 the pre-war sterling parity as 'the greatest mistake of my life'.)[1]

This simplified account of Britain's difficulties after the 1925 return to the gold standard provides a useful example of the domestic difficulties which can face a country on the gold standard.

---

[1] Sir Robert Boothby, BBC broadcast, 1973.

Drawbacks of the gold standard: 2. the liquidity-confidence problem
A possible stress area for any fixed exchange rate system is that of inadequate 'liquidity', that is, foreign exchange reserves. In the case of the gold standard the root of this difficulty lay in the shortage of gold. In the nineteenth century gold production had increased rapidly, particularly after the Californian gold discoveries of 1849, and the development of the cyanide refining process for South African gold in 1895. In the 1920s however gold production was one-third lower than in pre-war years, and countries' gold reserves now threatened to be insufficient for the gold standard to work properly.

One way of countering this gold shortage would be to introduce a 'gold bullion' standard (sometimes referred to as a 'partial' gold standard), under which central bank notes would no longer be freely convertible into gold coins by their holders, although they might still be converted into gold bullion bars of a minimum size by importers needing to make payments abroad. In the case of Britain, which adopted the bullion standard when it returned to gold in 1925, this minimum size was 440 ounces (worth about £1700). Thus for the man in the street in Britain the day of the full (domestic) gold standard was now over. It has been estimated that more than one half of the increase in the central bank's gold reserves between 1913 and 1938 was accounted for by the transformation of gold coins into centrally-held bullion reserves.

A second method of economizing on the use of gold was to adopt a 'gold exchange standard', in which countries' central banks would hold a proportion of their foreign reserves in the form of national currencies tied to, and convertible into, gold. The pound sterling had long performed a reserve currency role, and following the 1922 Geneva Conference the system was extended to include other currencies, particularly the dollar.

However, there is a problem with a gold exchange standard: if, due to the need to finance expanding world trade, reserves of gold are growing more slowly than the total of reserve currencies, the ratio of the 'reserve currency' countries' short-term liabilities to their gold reserve assets will get steadily worse and worse. (In fact the main way in which such countries can provide reserves for other countries is by running a balance of payments deficit.) Moreover, due to the shortage of effective reserves, some countries will be tempted to hoard gold by pursuing selfish bad-creditor policies[1] – thus making the liquidity problem of the gold standard even more serious.

A 'confidence problem' is also likely to develop. Money will function efficiently, whether domestically or internationally, only if there is confidence in its acceptability. If there is a loss of confidence in one of the world's reserve currencies, there will be speculative conversions of that currency into gold, which will lead to a fall in the gold reserves of that country, thus undermining the status of its currency still further.

In the 1920s it was the pound which often ran into trouble as a reserve currency. Before the First World War Britain's balance of payments had been strong, and short-term funds were readily available to match sterling's reserve currency liabilities. After the War however, Britain's balance of payments was too weak fully to support the reserve currency status of the pound, and whenever confidence in the pound slackened Britain's gold reserves became very vulnerable to heavy speculative pressures, as speculators turned pounds into gold.

There were now several reserve currencies and three major world financial centres – London, New York and Paris. This too increased the vulnerability of the gold exchange standard to speculation, as confidence faltered first in one reserve currency and then another, with swings of 'hot money' taking place from one financial centre to another, putting heavy pressures on the gold reserves of the countries concerned.

Drawbacks of the gold standard: 3. the adjustment problem
In order to deal with a persistent balance of payments deficit it is necessary for a country to take steps to restore the foreign competitiveness of its goods. One method is by devaluing its currency (p. 20). Under the gold standard this form of adjustment was ruled out. The other method is to deflate domestic costs and prices. As we saw in the case of Britain in the 1920s this might involve substantial reductions not just in prices but also in real income and employment. Thus there was under the gold standard no really effective 'adjustment mechanism' for a country's balance of payments.

Matters were made worse by the fact that the gold standard

---

[1] p. 89.

contained no effective pressure to stop surplus countries from pursuing selfish bad-creditor policies. For example, when France returned to the gold standard in 1925 it deliberately undervalued the franc in order to make its goods very competitive, and it soon began to run a balance of payments surplus and build up large foreign reserves. At first these were in the form mainly of reserve currencies, but from 1928 further increases in France's reserves were in gold. In 1931 the central banks of the United States and France adopted a policy of converting their holdings of reserve currencies, including sterling, into gold, which put great pressure on Britain's gold reserves.

One reason for these bad-creditor policies was the fear that national currencies held as reserves might sooner or later be devalued; that is, that the gold standard would in effect collapse. The result was to undermine the status of large amounts of international reserves and to weaken the gold standard still further.

Because of this asymmetry between the pressures on deficit and surplus countries, the gold standard tended to have what was called 'an inherently deflationary bias' on world economic activity. The failure of the system to provide scope for effective balance of payments adjustment was sometimes called the 'tyranny of the gold standard'.

The collapse of the gold standard

All three difficulties – unemployment, the liquidity shortage and the adjustment problem – contributed to the unsatisfactory working of the gold standard. Its final collapse in September 1931, was triggered off by the financial crisis which developed in the United States in 1929. For much of the 1920s, investment, business activity, and profits in the United States had been running strongly and this had led to steadily rising share prices. But by 1929 investment opportunities there were, at least for the time being, declining. Business profits now fell and heavy speculative sales of securities set in, culminating in the dramatic collapse of share prices on Wall Street in late October 1929, which reinforced the disinclination of businessmen to invest. Also, many stock exchange speculators, as well as businessmen and farmers, had borrowed heavily to finance their activities and now found themselves unable to repay their debts. This resulted in widespread banking failures – over 900 banks failed in the United States between 1930 and 1933. This further affected the decline in consumer and investment spending, so that production and employment fell heavily.

The financial crisis in the Unites States soon spread to other countries. First, short-term American investments, particularly in Europe, were diverted back to the United States, first to feed the Wall Street speculation, and then to try to meet the financial difficulties following the crash. Secondly, the decline in United States imports spread the depression into other countries via their export sectors, resulting in a world-wide multiple contraction of trade and employment (p. 89).

Major international financial difficulties followed. In May 1931 two important banks in central Europe, which had been relying on short-term American capital, closed their doors. A panic set in as governments and individuals rushed to convert uncertain currency assets into gold. Much of this selling centred on London, whose financial position since the First World War had never been strong, and which was known to have lent to continental banks to try to help them off-set the withdrawal of American and French funds. The pressure on Britain's gold reserves now became intense. In September 1931 Britain left the gold standard when the government decided to suspend the rights of residents to ship gold abroad. The pound was allowed to float freely on the foreign exchange market, and quickly depreciated.

A number of countries, including Canada, India, Denmark, Norway and Sweden, followed Britain off the gold standard. Others, including the United States, Germany, France, Belgium, Holland, Italy and Poland, stayed for a time on gold and became a 'gold bloc'. There were now therefore two quite distinct exchange rate systems operating: fixed rates, used by the gold bloc countries; and floating rates used by Britain and certain other countries. Inside this latter grouping, a number of countries having strong ties with Britain adopted fixed exchange rates with the floating pound, and became a 'sterling bloc' (after 1939, with some changes of membership, this became the Sterling Area).

Early in 1933 the United States adopted a floating exchange rate for the dollar, but in 1934 it went back to the gold standard. The dollar was now set at only 59 per cent of its former gold parity, in order to restore the competitiveness of United States products against those of other countries, many of whose currencies had depreciated. In 1936 France itself, now suffering from the effects of an over-valued currency, left the gold standard and allowed the franc to depreciate. As the shadow of the Second World War approached, more and more countries were experimenting with floating exchange rates, and the day of the gold standard seemed to be well and truly over.[1]

Summary

1. The gold standard was based on the convertibility, at fixed rates, of national currencies into gold. This enabled international payments to be financed by gold movements between countries.

2. The central bank of a deficit country would find itself losing gold; as a result of the contracted domestic money supply the country concerned would undergo deflationary pressures. This would in time restore its products' competitiveness and lead to a recovery of the country's balance of payments, and a cessation of the gold out-flow. A converse sequence of events would take place in the case of a surplus country gaining gold.

3. A serious drawback of the gold standard was that a deficit country undergoing deflation might experience prolonged unemployment – as Britain did after 1925.

4. A second drawback ('the liquidity problem') arose from the world shortage of gold supplies, once the major gold discoveries of the nineteenth century were over. In the 1920s countries tried to deal with this shortage by adopting the gold exchange standard, in which the pound and the dollar were reserve currencies, supporting the role of gold. However this led to a 'confidence problem' in the form of severe speculative pressures on certain countries' gold reserves.

5. The third drawback was that under the gold standard countries' exchange rates were rigidly fixed. This made it difficult for countries to regulate their balance of payments positions: the 'adjustment problem'.

6. These drawbacks led eventually to the collapse of the gold standard, in 1931.

---

[1] See V. S. Anthony, *Britain's Overseas Trade*, Heinemann Educational Books, 1969, Chapter 3.

5
THE EXPERIENCE OF THE INTERNATIONAL MONETARY FUND SYSTEM

The origins of the International Monetary Fund

In the last chapter we studied the workings of the gold standard. It was, we saw, a very rigid type of fixed exchange rate system and its collapse in 1931 was due, in the end, to its inability to deal with two inter-related problems. These were the adjustment problem (the need of a country with a payments deficit or surplus to take effective measures to restore balance of payments equilibrium); and the liquidity-confidence problem (the need of a country to hold sufficient foreign exchange reserves to defend its exchange rate while it deals with its balance of payments).

After the gold standard collapsed a number of countries, including Britain, for some years tried out floating exchange rates. These however did not work well and after the Second World War countries got together and formed the International Monetary Fund, which was intended to be the basis of an improved fixed exchange rate system. The IMF had its origins in discussions which took place, mainly, to start with, between Britain and the United States, and which culminated in the Bretton Woods Conference, in the United States in 1944. The intention was to develop a fixed exchange rate system which would be more flexible than the former gold standard but more stable than the erratic floating exchange rates of the 1930s.

The aim of the IMF: 'managed flexibility'

The workings of the IMF, which began in 1947, were based on the following principles.[1] First, all member countries should, even when in balance of payments difficulties, allow their currencies to be freely convertible and refrain from using exchange controls. The aim of this provision was to promote multilateral payments and trade between member countries.

---

[1] W. M. Scammell, *International Monetary Policy*, Macmillan, 1970, Chapter 6.

Secondly, stability of exchange rates was to be sought through the 'adjustable peg' type of fixed exchange rates. In this system members would use fixed exchange rates, but major changes in these would be allowed from time to time to deal with fundamental balance of payments changes. Minor changes in exchange rates, up to 10 per cent, would not need IMF approval. The adjustable peg was thus intended to provide member countries with an effective balance of payments adjustment mechanism. The values of member countries' currencies were to be defined in terms of a gold value which would in turn determine exchange rates between the various currencies (as under the old gold standard). Each country's central bank would use its foreign exchange reserves to maintain, within a narrow band, its currency's exchange rate (as explained on p. 16).

A third provision of the IMF was the setting up of a large multinational foreign exchange 'pool', on which a country with a temporary payments deficit might draw to reinforce its own reserves, so as to help maintain its exchange rate. This feature was aimed at overcoming the liquidity-confidence difficulty of the gold standard days. Each member was to pay into the pool a quota, one quarter being in gold and the remainder in its own currency. The member then had an automatic right to 'purchase', in exchange for its own currency (that is, to draw on), the currency of other members up to 25 per cent of

TABLE 5.1 DRAWING RIGHTS AT THE IMF

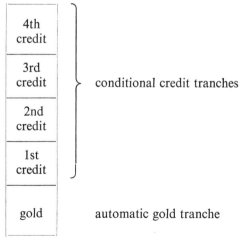

its own quota. This was called the gold 'tranche' (i.e. 'slice'). A member might then make up to four further drawings (the credit tranches) at increasing rates of interest, provided that, in the IMF's opinion, the member concerned was likely to use economic policies suitable for dealing with its balance of payments problem. In effect therefore a member country had potential drawing rights on the Fund up to 125 per cent of its quota. When its balance of payments deficit had been dealt with, the country in question would, within an agreed time limit, repay its drawings on the Fund.

A fourth feature, which we may briefly look at, was the IMF's scarce currency clause, designed to affect any country with a persistent balance of payments surplus. Normally deficit countries would soon experience a shortage of a surplus country's currency and would try to purchase it from the IMF pool. Under the scarce currency clause the Fund was allowed to 'ration' the scarce currency according to the needs of deficit countries. The effect of this restriction was to limit the demand by other member countries for the surplus country's exports and so, to some extent, to exert a discipline on it to reform its balance of payments policy.

To sum up, then, the IMF (or Bretton Woods) system was designed to be an adjustable peg system of convertible currencies, supported by access to a central international currency pool. In effect it was a more flexible type of gold exchange standard and was intended to be a compromise between the extremes of, on the one hand, the rigid unemployment-prone gold standard and, on the other, the erratic floating exchange rates of the 1930s. It is therefore often called the 'managed flexibility' exchange rate system.

How well did the IMF system work? A fair answer would probably be – 'reasonably well up to about 1960, but with increasing difficulty after that'. We shall begin by looking at the early years of the IMF.

Hard currencies and soft currencies

The IMF started collecting gold and currency from member countries, and accepting par values, in 1946, and began operating in 1947. One early task the IMF faced was to try to enforce the provision of convertibility for currencies, for during the Second World War most countries had introduced exchange controls. Achieving convertibility turned out to be a slow process. It had been foreseen that there would probably have to be a transitional period after the War during which some member countries would need to retain exchange controls while their economies, and balances of payments, were recovering from the effects of the War: during this time the IMF scarce currency clause would probably need to be activated. What was not foreseen was how serious the economic effects of the Second World War would be in most European countries, or how lasting their balance of payments difficulties.

First, there were the effects of the physical damage to Europe's infrastructure, including its means of transport and communication. Secondly, there had been considerable destruction of industrial capital. Thirdly, for various reasons, including war-time destruction and post-war politics, eastern Europe was no longer able to fulfil its pre-war role as a supplier of foodstuffs and raw materials, and the western European countries therefore found themselves paying high prices for imports of primary products from elsewhere. Fourthly, some European countries had sold off large foreign investments during the War – or had had them partly destroyed, as in British Malaya and the Dutch East Indies.

For all these reasons western Europe's capacity to produce, and export, manufactured goods, and its demand for imported primary products and capital goods, were both very inelastic. It would therefore be difficult to determine, for any given country, a 'correct' exchange rate which would balance the supply of exports against the demand for imports and so bring about balance of payments stability.

As the United States and Canada, having escaped the full effects of war, were now the main sources of supply for many goods which Europe desperately needed, most western European countries found themselves with a particularly heavy demand for dollars. To ration the demand for dollars the European countries used exchange controls, making their currencies inconvertible.

A distinction therefore came to be made between 'hard currencies' (those of economically strong countries like the United States) which were freely convertible, and sought after; and 'soft currencies' (those of most of the war-affected countries), which were weak, not much in demand and inconvertible. As a country operated exchange control it would find its reserves gaining some currencies and losing others. In a world of freely convertible currencies this would not matter since a balance of payments surplus with one country could be used to offset a deficit with another. But in the post-war world a country with a surplus of soft currencies, say French francs, could not use them to finance imports for which payment had to be made in a scarce hard currency – for example, imports from North America.

This meant that, for the time being, the part of the IMF pool which consisted of soft currencies was of little use for countries in balance of payments difficulty wishing to reinforce their foreign exchange reserves.

The United States found an answer to the dollar problem through Marshall Aid. Under General Marshall's plan very large amounts of dollar aid were made available to European countries between 1948 to 1952, to enable them to import goods which they needed to help build up their economies. The result was that in a few years many European countries had recovered so well from the war that their currencies became strong enough to stand up on the foreign exchange market without the support of exchange controls. Convertibility between the European currencies was achieved by 1958 through the European Payments Union, and general convertibility for these currencies and those of many other IMF member countries by 1962. By that time the western European economy was in a generally healthy condition and the world dollar shortage was a thing of the past.

The 1947 sterling crisis
An interesting exception to the general picture of inconvertible currencies was the freeing of the pound from exchange controls in the summer of 1947. After the war, Britain's economy was very weak, for it was not only sharing the economic problems of the rest of Europe, but was also saddled with large foreign war debts. In 1945 lend-lease dollar war-aid stopped and as a replacement Britain asked the United States for a loan of over £900 millions. In return the United States persuaded Britain to lift its exchange controls on sterling and make the pound convertible on current account transactions, by July 1947.

The experiment was a complete failure. In addition to those foreigners who were earning sterling from exports to Britain being able to convert their pounds into dollars, it also proved possible for many other sterling holders (with the connivance of their central bank) to turn their pounds into dollars. In a dollar-hungry world the pound became a quick and easy route for acquiring dollars. The drain on Britain's dollar reserves became so large (contributing incidentally to the vulnerability of sterling in the 1949 crisis) that on August 20, 1947, convertibility of sterling had to be suspended after only five weeks. It was eleven years before the attempt was repeated – successfully.

Disorderly exchange rates

Another task facing the IMF in its early years was to introduce orderly exchange rates between member countries' currencies. One problem was disorderly 'cross-rates'.[1] To take an example, suppose the official exchange rate of sterling was £1 = $4.00, but the sterling-lira and dollar-lira direct exchange rates were such that the 'cross-rate' between sterling and the dollar was, say, £1 = $2.60. This would encourage British exports for the United States market to go first from Britain to Italy, and then to be re-routed from Italy to the United States. This would not only be a waste of resources but would also lead to Britain earning 'soft' lira and Italy valuable 'hard' dollars. Disorderly cross-rates affecting the Italian lira and the French franc were by 1949 ironed out through agreements between the countries concerned. But other examples of disorderly cross-rates persisted right up to the 1970s – especially those due to multiple exchange rates[2] used by various Latin-American currencies to regulate different categories of imports and exports.[3]

The other aspect of exchange rate instability was the erratic changes which took place in many currencies' exchange rates in the years after the war. The Greek, Hungarian, Polish and Italian currencies were repeatedly devalued while the Canadian dollar and the Swedish crown were revalued upwards in 1946, as was the New Zealand pound in 1948. Then there was the world-wide rush of devaluations of soft currencies in late 1949, as Britain and the other countries undergoing post-war recovery tried to make their exports more competitive. After 1949 however the IMF principle of stable exchange rates operated pretty well.

Expanding the IMF's reserves facilities

During the 1950s world production and trade grew rapidly and it became evident that, if the risk of 1920s-type deflation, caused by insufficient international liquidity, was to be avoided, reserve facilities provided through the IMF would have to be substantially enlarged.

---

[1] B. Tew, *International Monetary Cooperation* 1945–70, Hutchinson, 1970, p. 20.
[2] S. J. Wells, *International Economics,* Allen and Unwin, 1969, p. 92.
[3] p. 85.

This was done in five stages by means of the following measures: stand-by credits; expanding the IMF currency pool; Basle Club 'swaps' by the central banks; The General Agreement to Borrow; and Special Drawing Rights. Let us examine each of these in turn.

Stand-by credits
A stand-by credit allows an IMF member which is under balance of payments pressure the right to draw on a stated amount of currency from the IMF pool for a certain period of time, with a possibility of later renewal. If the member's balance of payments quickly improves the stand-by credit may not in fact need to be used, but if support does become necessary the country concerned has the reassurance of knowing it can make a drawing on the Fund when necessary. A more economical use of the Fund's limited resources is thus possible. To obtain a stand-by arrangement a member has to provide a 'Letter of Intent', setting out its policy for correcting its balance of payments deficit, to be followed by close consultation with the IMF during the stand-by period. The first major use of stand-by credits was by Britain and France after their 1956 Suez military operation. Over the years the stand-by procedure has in fact become the most common method of access to the Fund's pool – rather than direct drawings.

Enlarging the IMF pool
The initial size of the Fund in 1947, at $9,000 millions, was arguably too low for two reasons. First, countries' own foreign exchange reserves were, with the exception of United States, now smaller relative to the volume of their imports than before the war. (The average proportion had dropped from 63 per cent to 45 per cent, and by 1957, due to expanding world trade, the figure was down to 34 per cent.) Secondly, most countries were now committed to full employment policies and were therefore less willing to deal with balance of payments deficits by using the deflation weapon. Thus they were more likely to need to draw on their foreign exchange reserves.

In 1959 members' quotas at the IMF were increased to a total of $14,000 millions. In 1966 the Fund's resources were enlarged to over $20,000 millions and in 1970 its size was increased further, to about $30,000 millions.

Basle Club swaps
The Basle Club developed at the time of the 1961 currency crisis which mainly affected the British, German and Dutch currencies.

Britain's balance of payments at the time was weak, due to the effects of the 1959 election boom which had increased inflationary pressures and reduced the competitiveness of British products. In Germany and Holland on the other hand, improving efficiency and strict disinflationary policies had led to a strong balance of payments. In March 1961 the German and Dutch governments took a correct good-creditor course and revalued their currencies upwards, by 5 per cent. Unfortunately, by exposing Britain's weakness, and highlighting a further possible revaluation of the mark and the guilder in terms of sterling, this led to heavy speculative sales of sterling, so that Britain's reserves came under severe pressure.

At one of the regular central bank meetings in Basle, the leading IMF countries agreed to try to defeat this speculation by swapping one another's currencies, so as to support the reserves of a member experiencing balance of payments difficulties. (Strictly speaking this arrangement was outside the IMF provisions, but since it involved the leading IMF members, it has been included in this section of the book.) As fast as speculation increased the reserves of, say, Holland and Germany, their central banks would provide their currencies in exchange for pounds to the Bank of England to enable it to support the pound's exchange rate. This plan was put into operation in 1961 – and succeeded. When it became clear that speculation was going to fail and that no devaluation would be forced, speculators covered their positions by re-buying pounds. By July the Bank of England had acquired enough foreign exchange to pay off its swap arrangements with Germany and Holland, together with some IMF drawings it had made; an IMF stand-by of £400 millions was however retained.

Further Basle-type anti-speculative rescue operations were used to defend the Italian lira in 1964 and the pound sterling in 1964 and 1966. In 1968 the central banks evolved a system of continuous recycling of currencies as a device to help protect currencies against speculation.

The General Arrangement to Borrow (*Group of Ten*)
The Group of Ten consists of the larger and richer IMF members, namely Belgium, Canada, France, Germany, Italy, Japan, Holland, Sweden, the United States, and the United Kingdom. The General Arrangement to Borrow which these ten countries set up after the 1961 currency crisis, allowed them to support one another's curren-

cies through a supplementary pool of about $6,000 millions which they contributed at the IMF. This auxiliary liquidity would not be available automatically but would require the consultation and approval of the group. The facility would be available only if the group decided that an IMF 'Letter of Intent' condition could be met – that is, a sound balance of payments policy by the country making the drawing, based, generally, on effective disinflationary policies. The GAB was used by Britain in 1964 and later, and by France in 1969.

Special Drawing Rights (paper gold)

The most fundamental measure taken by the IMF to improve international liquidity took place under the 1968 Rio de Janeiro agreements. These allowed the IMF to create and issue every year to member countries a new form of reserve asset known as Special Drawing Rights (sometimes called paper gold). The use of SDRs, which began in 1970 with an issue of $3,400 millions, was more than just a further step forward along the road of stand-by credits, enlarged IMF quotas, Basle swaps and the Group of Ten arrangements. For these measures, although important, merely increased what Professor Tew[1] has called 'liquidity-in-the-red'; that is they are forms of temporary, borrowed, liquidity which has eventually to be repaid. SDRs on the other hand, are 'liquidity-in-the-black'; they are *owned* by members (in proportion to their IMF quotas) and are, therefore, a permanent addition to the supply of international liquidity. Also, the IMF can decide to issue SDRs at whatever rate is needed to keep international liquidity in line with the growth of world trade (in the same way as the Bank of England can, and does, increase its fiduciary issue of notes in line with Britain's internal level of business activity).

The SDR system works like this. Suppose country A needs extra foreign exchange reserves to help support its fixed exchange rate, and decides to use the SDR facility. It will inform the IMF of its need for, say, $100 millions of foreign exchange and the IMF will in return tell A which member countries (generally those with a strong balance of payments position and ample reserves) have currency available. Country A can then use some of its SDRs to purchase currency from the countries in question. As SDRs exist only in an abstract form, in a special IMF account, the Fund need

---

[1] op. cit.

only, by means of a simple internal book-keeping entry, reduce A's holding of SDRs, and increase A's partners' holdings, by $100 millions.

One limit on the use of SDRs is that each country must retain an average of 30 per cent of the SDRs it has been allocated over the preceding five years. Another limit is to do with the acceptance of SDRs: any IMF member may decline to accept further SDRs from other members once its own SDR holding exceeds three times the amount of SDRs allocated to it by the IMF. Members selling SDRs pay the IMF, and members accepting them receive from the IMF, a small rate of interest. Participation in the scheme is voluntary – no member country is obliged to take up a particular issue of SDRs.

Due to the disturbed state of the world monetary scene, including the collapse of fixed exchange rates, the IMF suspended the issues of SDRs for 1973 and 1974.

Forms of first-line international liquidity

In the preceding sections we saw how successive reforms of the IMF arrangements, culminating in the SDR scheme, led to substantial increases in the supply of what might be called second-line liquidity available to countries through the IMF. Next, we need to look at the main element in international liquidity, that is, countries' own reserves of first-line liquidity. This has consisted of gold, together with dollars and sterling, which have been the main intervention currencies which central banks have used on the foreign exchange market to maintain fixed exchange rates.[1]

Let us first take the period up to about 1960. As far as gold is concerned, world reserves were at this time increasing, although rather slowly. Turning next to the dollar we find that it came into use as a reserve asset in two stages. First from 1947 to 1952 (at the time of the dollar shortage), the Marshall Plan led to a massive flow of aid in the form of dollars to Europe, some of which in fact accumulated as central bank reserves. Then, in the later 1950s, with the recovery of Europe and the weakening United States balance of payments, there was a flow first of gold and then dollars from the United States into the reserves of other countries. Sterling's status as a reserve currency goes back many decades, and after the Second World War, sterling gained added importance with the growth of

---

[1] p. 16.

Britain's foreign debts, in the shape of sterling balances held by Sterling Area countries (Case Study 2). At first these balances were not convertible outside the Sterling Area but when the pound became fully convertible they became a particularly useful reserve asset, earning a good rate of interest.

The liquidity-confidence problem of the 1960s
Turning now to the period after about 1960, we find that the post-war IMF (Bretton Woods) system, which was essentially a gold exchange standard, started to run into a serious liquidity-confidence difficulty. The problem was really the same as in the 1920s: against a background of steadily rising international trade, the world supply of gold was rising too slowly to support the rapidly expanding need for currency reserves. The result was that confidence in these began to fail. An important factor behind the gold shortage was the United States policy of keeping the world price of gold fixed at its 1934 price of $35 per ounce. The motive for this was to limit the scope for inflation inside the United States, whose domestic monetary system was partly gold-based; and to avoid disturbing the international monetary system by changing the price of its monetary base – gold. The effect however of the fixed price for gold was to make gold mining in South Africa and the other gold producing countries less and less profitable; also it encouraged hoarding of gold. The other side of the liquidity problem was the huge outflow of dollars from the United States, combined with the decline in its gold reserve, due to what had now become a large and chronic balance of payments deficit. (Between 1958 and 1967 the United States gold reserves fell by an average of nearly $3 millions *per day*.) This deficit was caused partly by the recovery of European exports and partly by the high rate of foreign investment, military spending and aid from the United States. In Britain the balance of payments difficulties of the 1960s were also leading to a weakening of confidence in the pound as a reserve currency.

Taking all these factors together it was only a matter of time before a crisis of confidence in the two world reserve currencies occurred.

The weakening of the dollar
Trouble set in for sterling with severe speculative crisis in 1964, 1966 and 1967 (Case Studies 1 and 2), leading eventually to the decision in 1972 to abandon a fixed exchange rate and allow the pound to

float instead. In the case of the dollar we can point to three stages in its decline as a reliable reserve currency. The first began in 1960 when, for the first time since the 1930s, United States short-term dollar debts exceeded the value of its gold reserves. In 1961 expectations of a possible dollar devaluation helped to trigger off speculative selling of dollars on a large scale, both by private individuals and central banks, against other currencies and gold. The second stage came in 1967, when the central banks' gold pool, which had been set up in 1962 to stabilize the value of the dollar in terms of gold, ran into trouble. The 1967 sterling devaluation also led to renewed speculative sales of dollars to buy gold, and between November 1967 and March 1968 the central banks were forced to supply some $3,000 millions of gold to hold the price of gold steady. In March 1968 speculative pressure became so great that the gold pool had to be abandoned. It was replaced by a two-tier scheme in which the $35 price was maintained only for gold sales between central banks; the price of gold on the private market was left to the forces of supply and demand.

In 1971 the third crisis stage for the dollar was reached. The United States balance of payments deficit was now so serious, and the build-up of dollar liabilities abroad so large, that the United States government decided it had no option but to suspend the convertibility of dollars into gold at the central bank level. And so, at one stroke, the post-war gold exchange standard disappeared, to be replaced by a 'dollar standard'. In fact, however, the change was not really so dramatic as this, for the United States had for a number of years been persuading the central banks not to convert the growing 'overhang' of dollars they were holding into gold. Another point to remember is that although the dollar was no longer convertible into gold at central bank level, that is, on an 'asset basis', it was still fully convertible into other national currencies on the world's foreign exchange markets: there was still 'market convertibility'.[1] There was, in other words, never any question of the United States introducing general exchange controls to prevent holders of dollars from changing them into other currencies; in this sense the United States dollar remained just as convertible as, say, the Swiss franc or the German mark.

---

[1] G. Haberler, 'Prospects for the Dollar Standard', *Lloyds Bank Review*, July 1972.

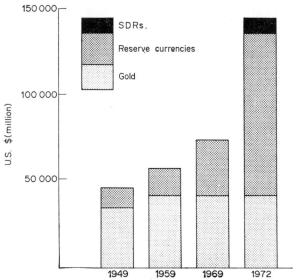

Figure 5.1   Main elements of world reserves 1949–1972

Summing up, then, we see that a fundamental liquidity-confidence contradiction had in the end undermined the effective working of the post-war IMF gold exchange standard. Whether the use of paper gold, that is SDRs, could provide a satisfactory alternative to national currencies as a form of international liquidity will be examined in Chapter 7. As for the future of the United States dollar itself as a reserve asset, much seemed to depend on two factors. First, to what extent the United States could control inflation, strengthen its balance of payments position and restore confidence in the dollar. And secondly, whether, and if so how, the enormous overhang of United States dollar debts abroad could be paid off or funded.[1]

The adjustment problem of the 1960s and early 1970s
The other main difficulty of the Bretton Woods system was its failure to provide a really effective adjustment mechanism for countries' balance of payments. Under the IMF's adjustable peg scheme the intention was that periodic re-alignments of exchange rates would

---

[1] p. 75.

enable countries to harmonize their balance of payments positions and avoid the rigidities of the old gold standard. Unfortunately, after about 1960 things began to go wrong. Furthermore, the failure of a number of countries to achieve balance of payments equilibrium threw added strain on the world's reserves of liquidity. There are several facets of the period worth studying: for example, Britain's balance of payments difficulties,[1] and the recurrent payments surpluses of Germany and Japan. Fundamentally though, most of these were bound up with, or affected by, one central feature, namely, the inability of the United States, the world's leading trader, foreign investor and supplier of reserve currency, to deal with its continuing balance of payment deficit. Did the fault lie with the United States itself, or with weaknesses in the international monetary system? The answer is both.

Let us examine the United States first. We may start by recognizing one crucial fact. This is that the United States' national product is very large indeed – so large that, compared with it, changes in its balance of payments are trivial. This meant that although the impact of the United States balance of payments deficit in the 1960s on the rest of the world was very serious, from its own point of view the effect was negligible. Even the increase in its foreign debts did not at the time cause the United States much concern. All this is very different from the position of, say, Britain, whose imports and exports are a high proportion of national income and for whom a balance of payments deficit is a serious matter. The United States therefore was not under very much pressure either to take steps to reduce inflation, such as a cut in general military and space programme expenditure, or to cut spending on the Vietnam War, which was badly damaging its balance of payments (in 1970 for example there was a deficit of $10,000 millions on United States government transactions abroad).

One factor behind the United States payments deficit was the relatively slow growth in its economic efficiency, compared with several of its foreign competitors, notably Germany and Japan. Year by year American products were running into severe competition both at home and abroad, for example, from Japanese and European cars, and Japanese electrical goods.

---

[1] Case Studies 1 and 2.

Problems of a pivot currency

Why did not the United States do what Britain, France and other countries might have done in similar circumstances – devalue its dollar to a lower exchange rate in order to restore the competitiveness of its goods, and make for a stronger balance of payments? This brings us to the crux of the matter. There are two points to consider here.[1] The first point involves the possibility of short-term movements in countries' exchange rates within the IMF fixed exchange rate bands. Before the 1971 Smithsonian agreement the 'band' was 2 per cent. This meant that the exchange rate between two currencies could, moving within their respective bands, change by up to 4 per cent (if one currency appreciated to the top of its band and the other depreciated to the bottom of its band). For a country in deficit on its balance of payments a 4 per cent depreciation of its currency could be of some assistance in restoring its balance of payments. However the exchange rate of the dollar, which was the pivot currency of the system, could only change by 2 per cent against any other currency. One advantage of a Special Drawing Rights pivot for the world's money system would be that the dollar would be free to fluctuate, if we take the post-1971 $4\frac{1}{2}$ per cent Smithsonian band, by a possible maximum of 9 per cent against any other currency.

The second disadvantage of the IMF arrangements from the United States point of view was that it was in practice impossible for it to use the IMF adjustable peg provision to reduce the official exchange rate of the dollar. Since member countries of the IMF expressed their exchange rates in terms of a gold-dollar valuation, there was therefore no standard against which the dollar itself could be devalued (or revalued). Suppose the United States authorities attempted to devalue the dollar by increasing the dollar price of gold. This would simply mean that other countries, whose currencies were tied to the dollar, would automatically increase their gold prices – so the exchange rate of the dollar would remain unchanged. Since no devaluation was available to the United States, the dollar seemed in the later 1960s doomed to remain over-valued and the crisis of confidence in it as a reserve currency to continue. The only way the United States could have engineered a devaluation of the dollar would have been by persuading (or bullying) the other main indus-

---

[1] G. Haberler, *op. cit.*

trial nations to revalue their currencies upwards against the dollar. Which takes us to the next point – the Smithsonian agreement of December 1971.

The 1971 Smithsonian Agreement

In the summer of 1971 the continuing United States balance of payments deficit led to renewed speculative sales of dollars, mainly against purchases of German marks and Dutch guilders; as a result the governments of these two countries decided to float their currencies temporarily in order to absorb, and deter, speculation. In August 1971 the United States government, faced with a seemingly indefinite prospect of an over-valued dollar and a payments deficit, took action to create for itself a bargaining position from which it could negotiate a devaluation of the dollar via an upward revaluation of the IMF parities of the other major currencies.

First, the United States suspended, officially, the convertibility of the dollar into gold between central banks; since this merely formalized the previous state of affairs, the effect of the move was mainly psychological. Secondly, the United States put an additional 10 per cent tariff on its imports, a move which particularly hit Japanese products, which had large exports sales in the United States market, partly on account of the under-valued yen.

In this uncertain situation most countries, including Britain, followed the lead of Germany and Holland by allowing their currencies to float on the exchange markets. After some months of informal negotiations – mainly amongst 'The Ten' – a stage was reached where a return to fixed exchange rates, based on a devalued dollar, became possible, in the shape of the Smithsonian agreement of December 1971. This agreement had two features. First, the maximum spread of a country's fixed exchange rate band was increased from 2 per cent to $4\frac{1}{2}$ per cent, thus allowing central banks more room for manoeuvre in the use of their reserves to resist speculation. Secondly, a wide-ranging set of upward revaluations of currencies against the United States dollar took place; at the same time, the dollar was formally devalued in terms of gold, the price of which was increased from $35 to $38 per ounce. The overall effect was that the United States dollar was devalued by about 9 per cent in terms of other currencies, compared with the pre-crisis situation.

TABLE 5.2   THE SMITHSONIAN CURRENCY REALIGNMENT OF
DECEMBER 1971

Currency	New central rate to U.S. dollar	Percentage revaluation compared with 30th April 1971
Belgian franc	44·8159	11·6
Dutch guilder	3·2447	11·6
French franc	5·1157	8·6
German mark	3·2225	13·6
Italian lira	581·5	7·5
Japanese yen	308	16·9
Swedish crown	4·8129	7·5
Swiss franc	3·84	13·6
UK pound	2·6057 ($ per £)	8·6

In the event, the United States balance of payments did not
improve significantly, and a further dollar 'devaluation' had to be

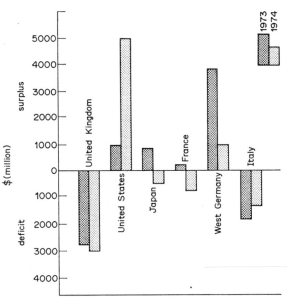

Figure 5.2   Balance of payments, current account, for 1973 and 1974
(OECD forecast).

negotiated early in 1973. Later in that year the United States government took the final logical step of arranging the floating of the dollar so that it would be free to depreciate to whatever lower exchange rate was necessary to permit a sound balance of payments. By then the United States was in fact moving towards a healthier balance of payments position, and for 1974 a current account surplus of $5,000 millions was being forecast – a big improvement on 1972 when there was a deficit of $8,000 millions. (This was after allowing for the effects of higher world oil prices, which were successively increased by the oil-exporting countries from an average price of 3 dollars a barrel in the summer of 1973, to over 10 dollars early in 1974.) The reader may care to check whether the balance of payments forecast proved correct!

Sticky exchange rates

Why were some creditor countries, such as Japan, reluctant to pursue good-creditor policies by allowing a devaluation of the dollar via an up-valuation of their own currencies? The main reason was their fear of reducing the international competitiveness of their industries, in case it should lead to slower economic growth and lower employment. If we turn next to the deficit countries (for example Britain in the mid-1960s), the reluctance in some instances to change exchange rates was partly political: there would be a loss of national prestige if, say, the pound failed to 'look other currencies in the face'.

After the 1971 currency crisis, attitudes about changing exchange rates became less doctrinaire. Surplus countries were more ready to follow the example of Germany, which had generally been prepared when necessary to increase the exchange rate of the mark. In the case of the countries which floated their currencies in this period there was of course a dramatic conversion to the principle of exchange rate flexibility! So, if the world does at some time return to the IMF adjustable peg system, sticky exchange rates will probably be much less of a problem than in the years up to 1971.

Summary

1. The International Monetary Fund (or Bretton Woods) system was based on three main features:
  (a) freely convertible currencies, to facilitate multilateral payments and trade.
  (b) access by member countries to a central IMF pool of foreign

currencies, as a source of second-line reserves, for dealing with short-term balance of payments difficulties.

(c) the adjustable peg provision for altering a member country's exchange rate, as an adjustment mechanism for dealing with a fundamental balance of payments difficulty. This feature was intended to avoid both the rigid exchange rate pattern of the former gold standard, and also the instabilities of floating exchange rates.

In essence the IMF system was an extended and modified gold exchange standard.

2. Up to about 1960 the IMF system made a valuable contribution to the post-war recovery of the world economy and the international monetary system.

3. After about 1960 the IMF system ran into the same sort of difficulties as the gold exchange standard did in the late 1920s.

(a) there was a 'liquidity-confidence problem': the dollar and sterling weakened and began to lose their acceptability as reserve currencies, as was shown by the dollar crises of 1968 and 1971, and the pound's difficulties from 1964 to 1968.

(b) there was an 'adjustment problem': a number of countries were unwilling (or in the case of the United States unable) to change their exchange rates in order to regulate their balance of payments.

4. In 1970 the IMF began to issue SDRs (paper gold). In 1971 the Smithsonian agreement led to a substantial realignment of countries' exchange rates. In spite of these two reforms, however, the United States and a number of other countries continued to experience balance of payments difficulties, which were accentuated by severe speculative pressures.

5. From 1972 an increasing number of countries adopted floating exchange rates to help deal with their balance of payments difficulties: the IMF regime had now – for the time being at least – come to an end.

6
THE EXPERIENCE OF FLOATING EXCHANGE RATES

The case for floating rates

We examined the theory of floating exchange rates in Chapter 1. Two main advantages have been claimed for floating exchanges. First, the risk which exists under fixed rates, of choosing and having to defend a 'wrong' exchange rate (for example the over-valued pound of the mid-1960s), is avoided, since the forces of supply and demand on the foreign exchange market determine the floating rate of exchange for a country's currency. A floating rate should therefore make possible an easier adjustment of countries' balance of payments positions than do fixed rates. Also, unlike fixed rates, floating rates cost very little in real resources to operate.

The other advantage of a floating rate system is that the liquidity problem of fixed rates should be avoided. Since a country is not committed to defending a given fixed parity it does not need to hold large official reserves of foreign exchange. At most, a country's central bank might however wish to hold a relatively small reserve of foreign exchange, in order to pursue a policy of buying and selling foreign currency on the market, to smooth out the range of exchange fluctuations.

Erratic exchange rates

Floating rates were tried by a number of countries in the early 1920s and again in the 1930s, as a result of which they in fact got a rather bad name.

One drawback was that exchange rates at times fluctuated quite wildly, and so increased the risks faced by businessmen and investors, which was bad for international trade and investment. This point can be examined in two parts.

1. There is the problem of changes in exchange rates due to low elasticities of demand for a country's imports and exports. If the sum of the two elasticities is not much greater than unity, exchange rate fluctuations could be substantial; while if their sum is less than unity, fluctuations in the rate could be cumulative and destabilizing,

thus increasing any balance of payments disequilibrium.[1] The evidence in fact suggests that the elasticities are often quite high. In cases where a deficit country has not experienced an improved balance of payments after depreciation (or devaluation), the reason has often been not low elasticities but the fact that it did not pursue the appropriate policies to reduce domestic 'absorption' – in which case inflation pressures continued to weaken the balance of payments despite the lower exchange rate.[2] Even where a country is exporting a good for which the general price elasticity is low, the elasticity *for that particular country's exported output* may be quite high. For example, the world demand for coffee is fairly inelastic, but if one particular country producing coffee were to reduce its price unilaterally, via depreciation of its exchange rate, its export elasticity of demand could be substantial. Case studies quoted by Sydney J. Wells[3] show a foreign trade elasticity of demand of 5·0 for all commodities excluding textiles, for the period 1954–56; and 6·0 for finished manufactures for the period 1955–59. Another set of estimates gave elasticities of 5·6 and 4·5.

2. The second element is the risk that short run exchange fluctuations will be exaggerated by the activities of speculators. There are at least three groups of institutions which are known to be able to move speculative funds quickly and on a large scale. These are multinational companies with mainly United States dollar budgets but having large foreign interests; large internationally-based commercial banks managing their own and their customers' capital; and various central banks in different parts of the world, including the sensitive Middle East area.

When a currency begins to depreciate, speculators may be tempted to sell it now, in order to buy it back more cheaply later at a profit. In doing so they will accentuate the fall in its exchange rate. Similarly an appreciating currency may attract speculative purchases, and so strengthen further.

The risk is that when a currency's exchange rate depreciates, this in itself will generate further depreciation as speculators sell it, and as exporters slow down sales and importers accelerate purchases

---

[1] p. 8.
[2] p. 24.
[3] S. J. Wells, op. cit. p. 183.

('leads and lags' speculation). So a vicious spiral could be set up in which speculators by their activities make their own expectations come true, rather in the manner of the 1929 Wall Street boom and crash. This artificially low exchange rate could lead to the so-called J-curve effect: until the volumes of imports and exports have had time to respond to the reduced exchange rate, exports would, for the time being, be too cheap to pay for the higher cost imports. Import payments and export earnings could therefore get out of line, thus causing a worsening current account deficit. (This time lag factor was one reason for Britain's very large balance of payments deficit in late 1973 at a time when international speculation was depressing sterling.)[1]

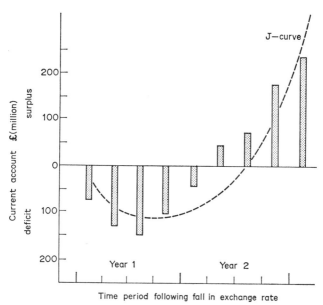

Figure 6.1   Hypothetical example of J-curve effect

An additional complication in recent years has been the development of the Euro-currency markets which have become an important

---

[1] p. 106.

form of private and semi-official liquidity and a potential source of speculative pressures (p. 110).

Economists who favour floating rates would disagree with fears about speculation and would point to the general fact that market operators make a profit by purchasing a currency when the rate is low and selling it when the rate is high. In doing this they tend to smooth out its market movements. Speculators who, by guessing wrong, destabilize the exchange rate will make losses and go out of business. Thus unless there is a permanent floating population of loss-making speculators (as perhaps there was in 1929 on Wall Street) speculation on a genuinely free foreign exchange market should reduce the amplitude of exchange rate movements. Also there are important real forces which limit the ability of asset holders, and of importers and exporters, to pursue speculative activities.[1] Where speculation leads to a fall in the exchange rate, asset holders will have fewer resources to draw on and the interest rate on speculative funds is likely to rise. Also exporters and importers will be exposed to the discipline of facing lower domestic and higher foreign prices. Thus unless the government undermines these real forces by pursuing inflationary policies which keep the rate of interest low and domestic prices high, destabilizing speculation should be of limited extent.

In any case it should not be overlooked that a fixed rate system may offer even better speculation opportunities than floating rates. The reason for this is that speculators operating in a fixed rate system are betting on a 'one-way option'. If, for example, speculators are selling pounds, a sterling devaluation will yield them a handsome windfall gain; if no devaluation takes place they can buy back pounds within the fixed rate band at little extra cost. In other words, under a fixed exchange rate system speculators are in a 'heads I win, tails you lose' position against the central banks who are trying to defend the currency in question. Under freely-floating rates there are no one-way options – the successful speculator makes his profit at the expense of the speculator who guesses wrongly.

It should also be stressed that firms working through a floating rate system can insure themselves against fluctuations by using the forward exchange market, as explained in Chapter 1. Under a float-

---

[1] H. G. Grubel, *The International Monetary System*, Penguin, 1970, p. 116.

ing system, forward markets tend to become well developed, covering contract periods up to several years and a considerable range of currencies. A second form of insurance is to borrow in the country where export receipts are due and deposit funds in a country where import payments are due. Thirdly, long-term contracts can be invoiced in terms of a strong currency and may include clauses which safeguard against cost changes arising from changed exchange rates. Fourthly, in the case of the really big trading and investment firms there is such a large spread of business around the world that the damaging effects of changes in exchange rates tend very much to cancel out. Finally, a central bank can, by buying and selling foreign currency unofficially on the exchange market as necessary smooth out the range of variation of the exchange rate (just as under a fixed rate system – but with the important difference that the unofficial ceiling and floor between which the central bank intervenes are variable, widely separated, and unknown to potential speculators).

False exchange rates

A second possible drawback of floating rates revealed by the pre-war experience, was that an unscrupulous government might push its currency to a 'false' exchange rate. For instance, in a time of recession a central bank could, by secretly selling home currency (and increasing its foreign exchange reserves), depress its exchange rate in order to boost exports and import-substitution and help overcome unemployment. In the 1930s a number of countries engaged in such competitive currency depreciation, though in the end their activities tended to negate one another and do more harm than good. It was to deal with this problem that the Tripartite Agreement of 1936 was signed between the major industrial countries to establish principles of fair exchange management. In a boom, on the other hand, the danger is that a country might be tempted to push its exchange rate *upwards* to try to 'export' an inflation problem.

The risk therefore is that the very logic of free exchange rates, namely that the market forces of supply and demand should determine the exchange value of a currency, would be undermined. Against this, the advocate of floating rates would reply that the risk of under-valuation or over-valuation of a currency also exists under fixed rates (for example the under-valued Japanese yen around 1970) and that the successful operation of any system of exchange rates must rest on international cooperation aimed at the pursuit of good-neighbour policies.[1]

Floating exchange rates and inflation

The third drawback of floating rates is potentially a very serious one. It is the risk that a country which has a relatively inelastic demand for imports, and which is also experiencing full employment, will find itself in a cumulative depreciation-inflation spiral. The sequence of events would be as follows. First, a depreciation of the exchange rate takes place, due perhaps to a seasonal trade deficit or to speculative capital movements. Whatever the cause, the result will be a rise in the price of imports, and thus an increase in the cost of living. The effect of this may be to trigger off a chain of wage increases which in due course will work their way through into further price rises. This will weaken the foreign competitiveness of the country's products, and its balance of payments, and lead to a renewed depreciation of the currency, resulting in an increased cost of living, further escalation of wage claims and so on. In this way a very dangerous hyper-inflation spiral might quickly develop.

The best antidote would be an effective anti-inflation programme via fiscal, monetary and incomes policies. In fact, sound economic policies are even more necessary under floating rates, where the price feedback effects of depreciation are so direct and rapid, than in a fixed rate system, where changes in the reserves tend to damp the immediate cost-push inflationary pressures of adverse terms of trade.

The Canadian experiment

We shall examine two instances of floating rates: first, the Canadian dollar float in the 1950s; and secondly, the experience of the floating pound from 1972. Now the first of these relates to a rather specific type of country (a primary producer highly vulnerable to changes in the terms of trade and foreign investment inflows). And the second took place at a time of great international monetary instability. Therefore we shall need to be cautious in drawing lessons from the two experiments.

---

[1] See p. 86.

Canada is a type of country which is very vulnerable to balance of payments pressures. First, many of its exports consists of primary products, the prices of which tend to fluctuate sharply. Secondly, Canada has relied for its economic development partly on foreign capital, the flow of which is sensitive to interest rates and profit expectations at the international level. In 1950, when the Canadian dollar was still on a fixed rate, both factors were moving in Canada's favour: on the balance of trade, the Korean war boom had sent the prices of Canada's commodity exports sky-high, while on the capital account a massive inflow of capital was being attracted into Canadian mining and industry. Its balance of payments became strong and a speculative demand developed for the Canadian dollar. The Canadian government was, quite rightly, reluctant to upvalue its dollar. One difficulty, always a problem with fixed rates, is to estimate a new equilibrium fixed rate: should it be changed by 5 per cent, or 10 per cent, or 20 per cent? The other difficulty was that when the world commodity boom broke, and Canada's export earnings fell, the Canadian dollar would weaken again – and so the new fixed rate would quickly become out of date and have to be changed yet again. It was therefore decided to float the Canadian dollar and allow the market forces of supply and demand to determine its value.

In general, the experiment, which continued until 1961, worked well.[1] Despite international pressures, Canada's balance of payments position remained stable, and changes in the Canadian dollar rate were quite moderate – from 1952 it remained within the range of 93 to 106 U.S. cents, and the rate from one quarter year to the next quarter never fluctuated more than 2 per cent. Also, there is evidence that speculation probably helped to reduce the fluctuation of the Canadian dollar. Nor was there any sign that foreign capital was deterred by the float.

In the late 1950s Canada's current account moved into deficit. It was also at this time experiencing deflation and unemployment. The logic of floating rates would have been to reflate the economy, while allowing the Canadian dollar to depreciate substantially. Eventually the government did decide to reflate, but it was reluctant to allow its dollar to depreciate. Instead it decided to use its foreign exchange reserves to support the dollar unofficially. This however provoked

[1] S. J. Wells, *op. cit.*, p. 194.

65

speculative sales of Canadian dollars and in April 1962 the Canadian government decided to adopt a fixed exchange rate for the Canadian dollar, which was now devalued to 99·2 U.S. cents. This triggered off a fresh wave of speculation; Canada's reserves fell quickly, and further deflation had to be undertaken to help the balance of payments. In the end the Canadian dollar had to be rescued by an emergency IMF operation.

Floating the pound in 1972

The experience of the floating pound in 1972 and 1973 was closely tied up with certain background factors, two of which had their roots before that time. One of these was Britain's inability, due to inflation pressures, to maintain a strong balance of payments position for more than a short time; ever since the mid-sixties the pound had been through periods of great weakness, leading to a large overhang of sterling balances debts abroad. A curious feature of Britain's inflation around 1972 was that it was combined with low output and substantial unemployment (nearly one million in the early months of 1972) – hence the term 'stagflation'. In order to stimulate economic growth the British government found itself embarking on a policy of

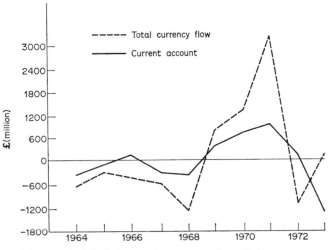

Figure 6.2   Britain's balance of payments since 1964

restraint of incomes and prices (to reduce wage cost pressures), combined with tax-cuts and an easy money policy to reflate domestic demand and output. In the event, no effective slow-down in wage cost inflation took place, but the rapid expansion of production began to put new pressures on Britain's balance of payments. In the early months of 1972 it began to look increasingly likely that sooner or later the exchange rate of the pound would have to be reduced.

The second background factor was the continuing weakness of the United States dollar, which had led to the gold crisis of 1968, and the dollar crisis of late 1971, and had made necessary the devaluation of the dollar in the Smithsonian agreement of December that year. In 1972 and 1973 the United States balance of payments and the dollar continued weak, which led from time to time to doubts about the other major international currency, the pound sterling.

The third factor which was to affect the sterling float was the introduction in April 1972 of a mini-European fixed exchange rate system known as the 'snake in the tunnel' scheme. Under this scheme the countries of the European Economic Community agreed to coordinate their economic policies so as to make possible the maintenance of jointly fixed exchange rates for their respective currencies within a band of only $2\frac{1}{4}$ per cent (the 'snake'). The 'snake' itself would then be kept within the standard $4\frac{1}{2}$ per cent IMF band (the 'tunnel') against the United States dollar and other currencies. The scheme was intended to be a first move towards eventual European monetary union, as well as helping the working of the EEC's common agricultural policy. Countries in the scheme agreed to support one another's currencies where necessary by joint central bank intervention, using their foreign exchange reserves. Britain and Denmark joined the scheme on May 1, 1972.

It was against a background of these three factors – balance of payments weakness in both the United States and Britain, together with the European 'snake in the tunnel' scheme – that the floating of sterling began in July 1972.

The pound leaves the 'snake'

In May 1972 the pound stayed comfortably off the floor of the EEC 'snake'. In June, however, Britain's trade figures were poor and there were also fears of a national dock strike. The fixed exchange rate obligation for the pound inside the 'snake' soon proved a powerful magnet for currency speculators looking for one-way options, who began to sell sterling against strong currencies like the German mark. The European central banks used their reserves to support the pound but the downward pressure on it soon became intense; about £1,000 millions left London in the final week of the crisis.

On June 23, 1972 the British government decided to abandon the 'snake in the tunnel' scheme, and the pound was allowed to float and find its own level. To counter further speculation an extension of exchange controls was announced to cover the whole Sterling Area, except for Eire. Meanwhile, despite the exit of the pound (and the Danish crown), the EEC 'snake' continued in operation.

In the weeks following the float the pound drifted down to about $2.45, a depreciation of 6 per cent. It remained at this level until mid-September when renewed fears about inflation, together with the continuing balance of payments deficit, led to a further fall in the pound, to $2.32 (an 11 per cent depreciation). After Britain's government announced the prices and incomes standstill in November 1972, the pound steadied at about $2.38.

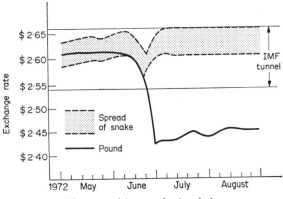

Figure 6.3   The pound leaves the 'snake'.

In the early months of 1973 the pound escaped the worst effects of international monetary instability, but in the summer, with continuing inflation and balance of payments difficulties for Britain, a sensational fall in sterling set in; in September the pound fell by 3 per cent in three days, to a level $18\frac{1}{2}$ per cent below its pre-float parity. For the rest of 1973 the pound strengthened only slightly against more currencies and remained weak against the United

States dollar. (Details on the sterling float are to be found in Case Study 3.)

The floating pound and inflation

Did the experience of the floating pound in 1972 and 1973 support or refute the case for floating rates? As always there are, among economists, differing points of view.

One danger was that higher import prices, caused by a depreciating pound, might become a catalyst for wage-cost inflation. However wage-cost inflation was also severe in countries such as Switzerland and Germany whose currencies' exchange rates went up at this time! Even if it was true that impulses from abroad were a factor tending to worsen inflation, the cases of Germany and Switzerland showed that the basic cause of inflation must lie elsewhere – very possibly, in the inability of countries pursuing policies of high taxation and high government spending to find ways of resisting aggressive wage claims.

Another factor behind Britain's inflation difficulties was the rise in world commodity prices. In 1973, Britain's terms of trade worsened by 18 per cent, which took, in the form of increased prices, about £2,000 millions out of the pockets of British consumers. If the terms of trade continued to worsen this fast, Britain would need its entire annual $3\frac{1}{2}$ per cent growth of national product simply to bridge the continuing trade gap. There was little doubt that the squeeze on real consumption brought about by the rise in world commodity prices was a more powerful catalyst for increased wage claims in Britain (and in other countries) than was a depreciating exchange rate. Thus there was no direct connection between the world boom in commodity prices and the depreciation of the pound – Britain's import prices would have risen under either system of exchange rates, fixed or floating.

Erratic exchange rates

The experience of the floating pound from 1972 also seemed to show that floating exchange rates mean erratic exchange rates. According to economists who favour floating rates, when a floating currency is under pressure speculation should tend to stabilize it, since speculators are supposed to base their actions on what the exchange rate will be in the longer run.[1] Yet this did not happen in the case of the

[1] p. 62.

pound, or indeed the other floating currencies, in 1972 and 1973. On the contrary, speculation seemed to be making the pound weaker, and less stable, than ever.

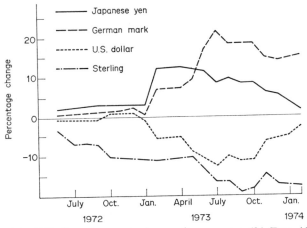

Figure 6.4   Effective changes in key exchange rates (21 Dec. 1971 as base).

This criticism however was ill-founded for basically it missed the main point, namely, *that although the pound was floating, other important currencies and currency groups, notably the EEC 'snake', were still on a fixed rate basis.* This co-existence of fixed and floating rates meant that the foreign exchanges were getting the worst of both worlds: sharply fluctuating floating rates were being fed by fierce speculative movements in and out of the fixed rate currencies. In other words the floating rate system was not getting a fair chance. (See Case Study 3 for further details.)

Secondly, this period was one of great economic instability due to: world-wide inflation, including the effects of rapidly rising primary product prices; anxieties about the effects of reduced and dearer oil supplies; and the ever-present risk of a major international recession.[1] Bearing this in mind it can be argued that the element of exchange rate flexibility introduced by the floating of the pound and various other currencies (including in 1973 the dollar) was surprisingly

---

[1] Due to go-it-alone policies (p. 89).

successful in absorbing so many international monetary shocks. Would the former IMF adjustable peg system have survived all the stresses of 1973? It seems unlikely.

The other question we need to ask is whether the floating of the pound and a number of other currencies increased business uncertainty. The answer appears to be, no. An investigation undertaken by Geoffrey Bell (*The Times*, May 16, 1973) among about forty international financiers and bankers showed that most of them welcomed the system of fluctuating exchange rates and found no really serious problems in conducting their business. A survey by *The Economist* newspaper during the short-lived 1971 sterling float came to similar conclusions. The point is that small but frequent changes in exchange rates may well be less damaging to international trade and investment, than the occasional, but relatively large, changes of fixed exchange rates.

When all the detailed discussion of floating exchange rates from 1972 is over, we should not forget what is perhaps the key issue. This is the will of countries to co-operate in pursuing mutually compatible good-neighbour policies. If floating rates, by virtue of their flexibility as compared with other exchange rate systems, improve the chances of this, their case stands. If they encourage or provoke international disharmony, their case falls. The next few years will show which.

Summary

1. Since the exchange rate of a floating currency is determined by the forces of supply and demand on the foreign exchange market, a central bank does not need to hold large supporting reserves of foreign exchange. In principle therefore this should obviate the liquidity problem, which fixed exchange rates system have suffered from.

2. The risk of a country having an over- or under-valued currency, should not occur with floating rates: the adjustment problem of fixed rates should thus be avoided.

3. Possible drawbacks of floating rates are:

  (*a*) fluctuations in exchange rates associated with inelastic demand patterns, or with speculation, may damage international payments and trade.

  (*b*) a country may covertly under-value its 'floating' currency (in order to 'export' unemployment); or over-value its currency (to 'export' inflation).

(c) if a currency depreciates substantially, increased import costs could theoretically trigger off a cumulative inflation-depreciation spiral.

4. The experience of the floating Canadian dollar in the 1950s provides no real evidence of these three drawbacks.

5. The experience of the floating pound after mid-1972 shows little evidence to support 3 (a) or 3 (b). However this period did see a sharply depreciating pound, which added to Britain's inflation difficulties; it also led, through the 'J-curve effect', to a widening balance of payments deficit.

6. It is difficult to draw firm conclusions about 3(c) from 1972 because of various complicating factors:

(a) the speculation side-effects of the EEC 'snake'.

(b) the rapid escalation of Britain's (and other countries') oil import costs.

(c) the world inflation in primary product prices in general.

7
PROPOSALS FOR WORLD MONETARY REFORM

Introduction

We looked in the last chapter at the experience of floating exchange rates. In spite of widespread doubts about their viability, floating rates came into increasing use for most of the leading currencies in the period from 1972. It may be, then, that the most radical reform of the post-war international monetary system has already taken place. If floating rates do prove permanent, the main scope for future development is likely to lie in measures for increased international cooperation to stabilize the forces of currency speculation.

There are however economists who would argue that the best bet for a future world monetary system still lies in an improved system of fixed exchange rates. There are two main alternative proposals here. The first is for a return to the gold standard, to be achieved by means of a very much increased production and use of gold, allowing the phasing out of unstable reserve currencies such as pounds and dollars. The other proposal is for a return to an IMF fixed exchange rate system in which the supporting role of pounds and dollars would disappear, to be replaced by a greatly increased use of Special Drawing Rights, issued on a really large scale. The new IMF system might also incorporate 'sliding parities' ('crawling pegs'), under which countries' official exchange rate would change frequently by small amounts, instead of in large sporadic jumps, as under the IMF's adjustable peg system.

A return to the gold standard

There is still support for a return to gold among some economists, particularly in France. It will be recalled that an important factor behind the death of the full gold standard in 1931 was the shortage of gold, which directly led to liquidity-confidence problems and which indirectly worsened adjustment difficulties. Under a new gold standard, therefore, steps would have to be taken to increase very substantially the world's supply of monetary gold. It is true that the geological facts cannot be changed and that, so far as is known, there will be no more major gold finds such as the Klondike. However

73

there remains, inside the existing gold-producing areas of the world, a great deal of low grade ore which it has not yet been profitable to mine. A necessary condition for making it profitable would be to increase the world price of gold (which was held at $35 per ounce from 1934 right up to 1968) in line with mining costs, which rose several-fold in this period.

During 1973 the free market price of gold fluctuated around $100 per ounce, compared with $35 in 1968 when the central banks' gold pool stopped operating. This meant that it became profitable for South African mines, which provide 80 per cent of the West's gold, to mine some lower grade ores; and the fall in gold output which had been taking place in recent years was arrested. However even at a gold price of about $100 a substantial increase in output would not seem likely. The South African government was still having to subsidize marginal low-grade ore mines and give tax-free concessions to new low-grade mines; however, completely unprofitable disused mines were being kept in working order in case it should pay to start them up later. What would be necessary therefore would be for the world's central banks (and therefore also private users) to buy gold at a really high price – say $200 an ounce. This would very likely stimulate an increased gold output in South Africa and in the other gold producing countries. It might also lead to a greater trade in gold from Russia to the West.

TABLE 7.1   GOLD-MINING OUTPUT, 1971

	(*metric tons*)
South Africa	1000
Russia	195
Canada	73
USA	56
Japan	22
Ghana	22
Australia	19
Philippines	19
Rhodesia	16

A second effect of a high gold price would be that every bar of gold in a country's reserves would be worth much more! In early 1974 the central banks were still valuing their gold reserves at the equivalent of 42 US dollars per ounce (though this arrangement did not seem likely to last much longer). A price of $200 per ounce would thus have quintupled the value of the gold element in countries' reserves. It would also have allowed the United States, which still held 13,000 tons of gold, to buy back at a stroke its entire overhang of dollar debts abroad and put an end to the United States dollar's vulnerable position as a world reserve currency. (This would not however apply to Britain's meagre gold reserves.)

A third effect of a higher gold price might possibly be a cut-back in the industrial demand for gold (for example in dentistry and satellite technology), which at present takes about half of the gold production, thus making possible a re-allocation of supply into monetary uses.

Fourthly, a really high gold price might discourage or even reverse the private hoarding of gold, which has been going on on a large scale for many years. It has been estimated that around 1973 gold was being smuggled into India at the rate of $700 millions per year and that the stock of privately hoarded gold in France alone then amounted to $1,300 millions!

The case against gold
There are however strong arguments against the back-to-gold approach. First, the real (opportunity) cost of using gold is very great. After all, the cost of producing $1 million of say SDRs is negligible, but the cost of producing an equivalent amount of gold (about one large suitcase full) is $1 million! Moreover, the human costs involved in gold mining are very great – on average 500 miners are killed annually in South African gold mines and many more injured, in very difficult working conditions.

Another problem is that if countries agreed to fix the gold value of their currencies permanently it is difficult to see (bearing in mind what happened in the 1920s) how really fundamental balance of payments adjustments, reflecting long-term changes in international comparative costs, could take place effectively. Yet if changes in currencies' gold parities and exchange rates were allowed to take place these would almost certainly be anticipated by speculators, and would lead to enormous pressure on countries' gold reserves.

A third and related difficulty would be estimating the level at which the new gold price should be fixed, in order to provide the right expansion of gold production, and reserves, to match the expected growth of world trade. Increases in the price of gold, in terms of national currencies in general, would very likely prove necessary, but the effect would be to encourage speculative sales of currencies.

The fourth snag is the political factor – a higher gold price would benefit the main gold producers, which are South Africa and Russia. It would also give a windfall gain to countries like France, which has persistently pursued a policy of building up its central reserves of gold, at the expense of other countries' holdings.

In short, going back to gold would be a difficult, many-sided decision and the lack of a straightforward balance of payments adjustment mechanism could prove a fatal handicap. To this, the advocate of a return to gold would reply 'only gold is trusted': without an international currency in which there is real confidence, no international monetary system can succeed.

Expanding the use of SDRs

The other proposal for a reformed fixed exchange rate system would be to improve the IMF system by basing its workings on a greatly increased use of SDRs. As we saw earlier, the IMF system was in effect a gold exchange standard, in which national currencies supported gold as the basis of the system. We saw too that this type of system contains a contradiction: if the supply of reserve currencies expands rapidly they weaken in acceptability, but if they remain strong, it will be at the expense of their availability. The introduction of Special Drawing Rights in 1970 was intended to be a way out of this dilemma, since the status of SDRs, which are acceptable internationally by prior agreement, and nominated (but not convertible) in gold, is not tied to the balance of payments fortunes of the United States or any other reserve currency country. We examined the main outline of the SDR scheme earlier (p. 48). What we shall now do is first, examine briefly possible weaknesses of the SDR scheme; and secondly, indicate how the role of SDRs might be rapidly expanded in the next few years.

One shortcoming of the SDR scheme is that it does not put sufficient pressure on deficit and surplus countries to put their balance of payments positions in order. In the case of a deficit country there is a risk that it will use its allocations of SDRs to shore up its long term payments deficit, instead of using them as short run liquidity while it takes steps to improve its payments position. The risk of this happening is however somewhat reduced by the provision that any member must hold a balance of 30 per cent of the SDRs with which it has been issued.

What about a surplus country? Does the SDR scheme put pressures on it to avoid a persistent surplus? The answer at present is no. To counter this shortcoming it has been suggested that an absolute limit be placed on the amount of SDRs a country is allowed to keep. A country which accumulates SDRs above its limit should have to deposit them at the IMF *and pay interest on them.*

A numeraire for SDRs

A second difficulty is to do with the value of SDRs. Initially SDR units were denominated in gold value, but if there was a free world price for gold some other measure of value (numeraire) would have to be found. One possibility is for each SDR unit's value to be based on a bundle of representative currencies. In the course of time some currencies would no doubt rise in exchange value, others fall, but these would tend to cancel out and the value of an SDR unit would remain stable. It might be desirable for SDRs to carry a high interest rate to make them an attractive asset, so that countries could be persuaded to accept really large allocations. Another possibility would be for the value of a unit of SDRs to be based on the values of a bundle of stronger currencies (like the German mark, and the Swiss franc). A third suggestion[1] is that the value of SDRs could be based on the value of a bundle of primary commodities such as coffee, tin etc. This would mean that in a time of world boom the value of countries' holdings of SDRs would tend to increase in line with the growing needs of world trade. Also this scheme could be based on issues of SDRs to countries which produce and hold stocks of primary commodities. Since many of these are among the world's poorer countries, the scheme would provide a source of aid for them, as their SDRs could be used to pay for resources from the developed countries.

SDRs and international aid

It would in any event also probably be necessary to make a massive once-and-for-all issue of SDRs to fund the huge overhang of unstable dollars and pounds at present held as reserve currencies by various

---

[1] N. Kaldor, 'Reserves on a commodity standard', *The Times*, September 8, 1971.

countries (for example at one stage in 1973 West Germany's central bank was holding $40,000 millions of United States currency). The United States and Britain would then pay interest on their dollar and sterling balances to the IMF and would pay off their debts over a long period.

Should a link be established between SDRs and aid to under-developed countries? The amounts of aid involved could be quite considerable. It was estimated by Lord Kahn,[1] that if, on the basis of a theoretical world issue of SDRs of $10,000 millions per year (compared with $3,000 millions issued annually from 1970 to 1972), the advanced countries were prepared to place one half of their share of $7,000 millions (that is, $3,500 millions) at the disposal of the World Bank, aid to the poorer countries could be improved by about 19 per cent and the advanced countries' contribution would increase from 0·83 per cent to 0·99 per cent of their GNP.

An argument against this approach is that the creation of SDRs by an international authority does not directly absorb the use of real sources in the advanced countries, yet does at the same time give poorer countries a claim on their resources – therefore the link scheme would add to the world's inflationary pressures and would be against the interest of all countries in the long run.

Also the scheme runs into the even wider question of whether cheap official aid is the best way of fostering economic growth in the poorer countries. Some economists would prefer a policy of much freer trade combined with more vigorous private investment flows. Doubts about a possible SDR aid-link scheme are put at their strongest by Peter Bauer:[2] 'although at present the credibility of governments and international bodies is at a distinctly low ebb, momentous powers of decision about the creation and distribution of super-national money are proposed for international organisations set up by governments patently unable to manage their own domestic monetary system'.

The Triffin Plan

A very ambitious plan for IMF reform was outlined in 1960 by Professor Triffin. It would mean giving the IMF the powers of a 'world central bank' which would freely produce and generate

---

[1] Lord Kahn, 'SDRs and Aid', *Lloyds Bank Review*, October 1973.

[2] P. Bauer, 'Inflation, SDRs and Aid', *Lloyds Bank Review*, July 1973.

deposits of a world 'fiat' currency, such as SDRs. In the first stage the initial supply of SDRs would be fully backed by gold and national currencies contributed at the IMF by member nations. In the subsequent stages of the plan the IMF would use open market operations to buy gold and national currencies on the world's foreign exchange markets. When a central bank's currency was purchased it would find itself credited with an IMF deposit of SDRs which it could now use as part of its reserves. The IMF could therefore create fresh reserves of fiduciary SDRs to expand with the needs of growing world trade. The reason why the Triffin plan was not put into operation is presumably that it would give the IMF very strong powers over member countries' economic policies. (For example it would decide which member countries at any particular time most needed, or deserved, further SDR supplies!)

Sliding parities
If an IMF system, based on the greatly extended use of SDR liquidity, is one day resurrected, would it be a good idea to replace the adjustable peg system by the looser form of exchange rate system known as a crawling peg (sliding parity)? In one version of this, a country would be allowed, if it had a balance of payments disequilibrium, to revalue or devalue its currency annually by not more than a given amount, say, 3 per cent. Its exchange rate would then be likely to change frequently but in small steps, instead of occasional but massive jumps, which offer such tempting opportunities for speculation. In a second version a country undergoing a changing balance of payments position would be obliged to change its parity automatically and continuously (perhaps even daily) on the basis of a moving average of past exchange rates over, say, the last three years. In either version provision would probably also be made for a somewhat wider exchange band around the parity than in the former IMF system.

Advantages of the automatic sliding system would be its freedom from political pressures plus the fact that it would put equal adjustment pressures on both surplus and deficit countries. The main risk would undoubtedly be that a country's crawling exchange rate might not be able to change fast enough to allow it to stabilize its balance of payments. If this happened massive one-way speculation would certainly develop, and the liquidity-confidence problem of the former IMF system would reappear. It may be doubted whether a crawling peg system would have successfully absorbed the international monetary shocks which were caused by the 1973 Middle East oil crisis. At worst therefore, a crawling peg might provide neither the flexibility of floating rates nor the stability of a really successful fixed-rate system.

A final point: would the world's gold mining industry collapse if the Bretton Woods system was restored, and gold demonetized? Probably not. As Professor Triffin explains,[1] 'The most likely prospect is that the evolution of gold prices [would] be similar to that of silver prices after the demonetizing of silver: rising prices on the private market, even though slowed down at first by huge private and official dishoarding from the excessive stocks inherited from the past.'

Summary

1. The adoption of floating currencies by many countries in the period from mid-1972 may well become formalized and permanent: if so, it will have been the most radical reform of the international monetary scene to have taken place since the setting up in 1947 of the IMF system.

2. It is proposed by some economists that if the world does reject floating rates and return to fixed exchange rates, a full gold standard system should be selected. A necessary condition for this would be a high market price for gold, so as to make profitable a greatly increased production of gold as a source of world liquidity.

3. Possible drawbacks of a 'return to gold' would be:

   (a) the human and economic costs of mining and using gold for monetary purposes are very high, compared with alternative forms of international liquidity.

   (b) changing countries' exchange rates would probably be difficult.

   (c) a high price for gold would have important political implications, for it would unduly benefit the two main gold-producing countries.

   (d) choosing the 'right' world price for gold would be difficult.

4. The other main proposal for international monetary reform is to restore a modified and strengthened IMF system.

   (a) liquidity-confidence difficulties might be overcome by phasing out the role of gold and the two reserve currencies and replac-

---

[1] *Lloyds Bank Review*, January 1974.

ing them by Special Drawing Rights, or multi-currency units, or by commodity-backed currency units.

(*b*) adjustment difficulties might be tackled by a more flexible use of the adjustable peg; or through sliding parities.

5. In essence, the real test of any proposal for world monetary reform is this: *will it provide the best opportunity and incentive for countries to pursue sound and mutually compatible policies?*

8
THE INTERNATIONAL ROLE OF MONEY

Money and specialization

Money is important, for it is a medium of exchange and a standard of exchange. These functions help the mechanism of exchange and thus the process of specialization. Secondly, money is a store of value and a standard of deferred payments, which greatly facilitate lending and borrowing, and saving and investment. These, in turn, are aspects of specialization, and thus link back with the two earlier functions. The wider the market within which money operates, the greater will be the extent of specialization, and the increased productivity and living standards which it makes possible.

However, the importance of money is not confined to the national scene. Money payments take place from one currency to another between countries, and this too has beneficial consequences. One of these is well-known: it assists the operation of international exchange and specialization, at a given time, along the lines indicated by the law of comparative costs. Moreover, when specialization takes place, cost conditions themselves change as output expands and the economies of mass-production are obtained. Thus the effect becomes one of creating, rather than merely exploiting, comparative cost advantages. The enlarged European Economic Community is intended to reap this kind of advantage.

It is evident, too, that the process of international specialization will be damaged by barriers which hinder the flow of goods and services between countries. These may be natural barriers, such as transport costs, or social, linguistic and institutional factors. Or they may be artificial barriers to trade, such as import (or export) tariffs, quantitative import (or export) quotas, or subsidies on domestic production or exports. However, the flow of international trade can also be endangered by restrictions on international *monetary* payments. We may, if we wish, think of trade transactions and money transactions as equal and connected, but opposite-moving, conveyor belt systems: a slow-down in the trade conveyor belt will lead to a slow-down in the payments conveyor belt. Conversely, any damage to the payments flow will cause a reduction in the trade flow.

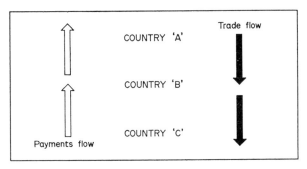

Figure 8.1

The growth-transmitting mechanisms

What is even more important however is the damage which a badly working international monetary system (or international trade system) can inflict on the dynamics of the *growth of international specialization* over long periods of time. Here we must refer to what Professor Harry Johnson[1] has called the 'growth-transmitting mechanisms'. Both of these take the form of international investment flows from developed countries outwards towards other parts of the world, in response to profit opportunities. These investment flows are themselves of course examples of international monetary payments, and are the counterparts of trade flows of capital goods. However the two mechanisms themselves depend for their effective working on an efficient international monetary system.

By economic growth is meant rising productivity and income per head, arising from investment in primary and manufacturing industry, in infrastructure services, and in the development of the human skills of workers, managers, engineers and scientists. As incomes rise and the scale of the market widens, so also do both opportunities for further investment in specialized large scale activity, and the capacity of the community to save on a scale to match this increased investment. Thus growth tends to become cumulative and self-reinforcing. This can be explained through the Harrod-Domar 'growth equation':

---

[1] H. Johnson, *The World Economy at the Crossroads*, Oxford, 1968, p. 11.

83

$$\frac{\triangle y}{y} = \frac{s}{g}$$

where $\frac{\triangle y}{y}$ is income growth; s, the community's saving propensity;

and g, its capital output ratio. In terms of this expression, there may well be a tendency for the rate of economic growth itself to accelerate as a country's savings rise and its capital-output ratio falls.

Much of the investment needed for economic growth comes, of course, from within countries. Here, we are concerned with the nevertheless important – and sometimes critical – role of investment which takes place from one country into another.

The first growth mechanism is triggered off by the increasing pressure of demand on natural resources in the developed countries. This induces firms in the developed countries to invest in exploiting resources in less-developed areas: United States investment in North Sea oil, and Japanese investment in Western Australian iron-ore, in recent years. The second growth mechanism comes from pressure, in the developed countries, on their high-wage labour resources. In the past this led to large migrations of workers from Europe to the New Continents; and more recently to Northern Europe from its economically dependent areas. In the absence of good labour mobility, however, private investment is particularly likely to flow from the developed countries into factories and other stages of production in areas of abundant low-wage labour. This low-cost production can then be exported so as to compete in the home markets of the developed countries. Moreover, it becomes profitable for firms in the developed countries to invest in educating and training labour in cheap-labour countries. This has been one motive for investment by United States firms in their European subsidiaries since the Second World War. There is little doubt that the evidence supports the validity of this theoretical explanation of growth transmission.

However, the growth transmission processes are very vulnerable to distortions and restrictions both in the international trade system and the international monetary system. In fact, political pressures in the developed countries for the deliberate use of defensive trade restrictions are likely to grow with time. This is because with continued economic growth and rising wages in the developed countries, their labour-intensive traditional industries will increasingly come under fire from cheap imports from the new growth countries: hence the plight of, for example, the cotton textile industry of Britain.

Equally, however, these growth mechanisms can be damaged if the international monetary system is working badly. Suppose, for example, that the growth process was causing fundamental changes in the international pattern of specialization and production, and thus causing considerable short-run pressures on some countries' balance of payments positions. Suppose, too, there happened to be a world shortage of international foreign exchange reserves such as gold, dollars and pounds. The effect of this shortage of reserves would then be to increase the risk of certain countries defending their weak balance of payments positions, and their reserves, by using restrictions on foreign monetary payments to block imports from their newer competitors, thus endangering the international growth process. A great deal is therefore at stake in the case of the working of the world's money system.

Types of foreign payments restrictions
One form of restriction is exchange control. This means that the residents of a country must hand over all their holdings and earnings of foreign currencies (for example from exports) to the central bank at the official rate of exchange. Residents may purchase foreign exchange (for example, to pay for imports) only with the permission of the central bank. By using exchange control the authorities of a country can thus restrict imports from competitor countries (except in cases where foreign suppliers are prepared to accept payment in an inconvertible currency which can only be used to purchase goods in the home country). In time of war, as a method of safeguarding scarce foreign exchange to pay for essential imports, exchange control is justifiable; but in peace-time conditions the long-term damage to specialization can be far-reaching. Exchange control may also be used to restrict not just imports but also capital movements on the balance of payments. If these are short-run speculative 'hot money' flows official intervention may perhaps be justified. But in the case of long-term investment between countries the risk to specialization and growth presented by exchange control should now be clear.

A second form of exchange control restriction is multiple exchange rates (multiple currency practices). These are in operation in most communist and a number of South American countries.[1] They are

---

[1] S. J. Wells, *op. cit.*, p. 89.

used to regulate various classes of imports and exports. For example in Columbia at the end of 1965 the government would buy foreign currencies from exporters of coffee at a rate of 8·50 pesos to the US dollar; but for manufactures the exchange rate was 9·00 pesos, for most other exports 13·50 pesos and for exports of services 18·27 pesos! Similarly the spectrum of exchange rates for imports varied from 9·00 pesos to 18·29 pesos per dollar.

Thirdly the international monetary system can be distorted if a country deliberately operates an artificially low exchange rate so as to make its products excessively competitive at the expense of other countries' foreign trade. This practice was a feature of international payments in the late 1930s, and it is a criticism which was levelled at Japan's policies around 1970. Conversely, a country might, theoretically, aim at an overvalued currency so as to absorb and 'export' an inflation problem.

We saw in Chapter 5 that it was an important aim of the International Monetary Fund to remove monetary restrictions and distortions, whether in the form of exchange controls, including multiple currency practices, or of disorderly exchange rates. Parallel to this, the World Bank, a sister institution to the IMF, also founded in 1947, has had the function of providing finance for investment projects in low-income developing countries; while the General Agreement on Tariffs and Trade (GATT), which began to operate in 1947, seeks to remove various trade restrictions, such as tariffs. The spheres of these three great international institutions are therefore closely related and they form a concerted attempt to bring about free-flowing conveyor belt systems for international payments and for international trade.

Good-creditor policies and good-debtor policies

Let us look at the matter from a slightly different viewpoint. An important test of any international monetary system is this: does it allow and encourage countries to pursue good-creditor and good-debtor policies on their balance of payments?

Consider the following (simplified) balance of payments table.

Debits		CURRENT ACCOUNT		Credits
£ millions			£ millions	
Visible imports	600		Visible exports	400
		CAPITAL FLOWS		
			Investment from abroad	200
	—	OFFICIAL FINANCING		
Change in reserves	—			—

We see that this (hypothetical) country is running a current account deficit of 200 and is therefore a debtor nation. However its deficit is being financed not by drawing on its reserves, which could eventually lead to a balance of payments crisis, but by an inflow of long-term foreign capital. Thus the value of its total currency flow is zero. The country is therefore *using its current deficit* to foster its internal economic growth. Its import surplus is probably accounted for by producer goods (e.g. mining equipment), which are being paid for at present by foreign money.

When these investments have matured a new balance of payments situation is likely to develop.

Debits		CURRENT ACCOUNT		Credits
£ millions				
Visible imports	400		Visible exports	440
Invisible imports (interest)	20			–
		CAPITAL FLOWS		
Repayment of investment	20			–
		OFFICIAL FINANCING		
Change in reserves	–			–

We can see that the earlier peak of imports is over and that the foreign capital is now in the process of being successfully serviced (on the invisible account) and repaid (on the capital flows account).

The country is able to do this out of higher exports (for example, iron ore) from the increased domestic production which the original inflow of capital made possible. In fact, the country has been pursuing a good-debtor policy. (Of course not all development projects go as well as this. For example, the foreign donors of the capital may misjudge the economic situation in the recipient country; or the latter may misuse and squander its borrowed capital resources, and therefore have no economic growth to show for it, or with which to repay its foreign debts.)

In practice, of course, there would probably be successive inflows of foreign capital over several decades before the country in question finally emerged from its debtor status. In due course it might itself become a 'creditor nation', with a continuing current account surplus which would allow it to invest capital resources in other (debtor) countries. The reader will be able to work out a simple balance of payments structure to illustrate a 'good-creditor' policy.

In a general sense, therefore, we mean by balance of payments equilibrium a situation in which a given country is pursuing the good-creditor policy or good-debtor policy which is appropriate to its situation. Balance of payments equilibrium *does not mean* a situation where each country strenuously pursues an exact current account balance, regardless of its state of economic development.

However, suppose the international monetary system is functioning badly: that countries are suffering from a shortage of foreign exchange reserves; that exchange controls are making many currencies inconvertible; that the exchange rates of major currencies are badly over-valued or under-valued; and that there is consequently little trust or co-operation between nations. In this kind of situation there is likely to be a mad scramble to defend balance of payments positions regardless of the true long-term interest of the countries concerned. The stronger or more ruthless trading countries may achieve a position of the kind shown below.

Debits		CURRENT ACCOUNT		Credits
£ millions				£ millions
Visible imports	600		Visible exports	1400
Invisible imports	100		Invisible exports	200
		CAPITAL FLOWS		
Investments	–			–
		OFFICIAL FINANCING		
Increase in reserves	900			–

This country is pursuing a bad-creditor policy. It is not helping itself, since its rapidly rising foreign exchange reserves are a sterile asset; it is not helping less developed countries, which it is starving of foreign capital; and it may be damaging the position of other economically developed countries, which it is preventing from achieving a natural creditor-investor status. The longer the situation continues, the more distorted the international monetary system is likely to become and the worse the pressures placed on countries with a vulnerable balance of payments position, low foreign exchange reserves, or a liberal balance of payments outlook. The reader will be able to work out a simplified balance of payments structure illustrating a 'bad-debtor policy'. It must be added, however, that not all bad-debtor positions are a result of general unfavourable external pressures of the kind we have mentioned: it is possible for a ship to run off course in a calm sea under a clear sky – as Britain's 1964 balance of payments difficulties showed![1]

Beggar-my-neighbour policies

Finally, let us take a look at the cumulative damage which can flow from a country pursuing unsound economic policies. Take, for example, a country experiencing a business depression, which causes a substantial reduction in its imports. Since one country's imports are another country's exports, other countries will find their exports falling. Suppose the first country's (A's) imports have fallen by 10 units; then it may well be that other countries, in order to adjust their balance of payments and protect their foreign exchange reserves, will have to cut their imports, including those from A itself, by,

---

[1] Case Study 1.

perhaps, in total 60 units. This is because under the regulations of the GATT organization, the other countries are not allowed to impose specific import restrictions on A itself. They must therefore adopt policies which reduce imports from one another as well as from A.

Also, if these other countries use deflationary policies to reduce their imports, their national incomes will shrink by a multiple of their import reductions; if their marginal propensity to import is say, one-fifth of changes in their national income, their collective national incomes will need to fall by 300 units. So the original 'infection' of A's beggar-my-neighbour policy will have spread and multiplied through the international community.

How does the international monetary system come into all this? In two ways. First if A's trading partners own, or have access to (for example from the International Monetary Fund), adequate foreign exchange reserves, they can delay their responses and give A time in which to try to reflate its economy. If, secondly, A does not succeed in doing this, exchange rate changes can come into play: the other countries can attack their balance of payments deficits (caused by A's business recession) by jointly devaluing their currencies by the same amount. This will make their products more competitive against A's and will enable them to achieve a balanced foreign payments position with A. However the relative values of their currencies *against one another* will remain the same and so the mutual trade reduction between them which we examined above would no longer need to take place. (The point may also be made that if A had had substantial foreign reserves in the first place it might have been more willing to avoid a recession.)

Actually, this is very much the significance of what happened in the case of the Japanese yen 'revaluations' and United States dollar 'devaluation' in the period from 1971 to 1973. It is for these reasons that exchange rate flexibility was a key provision (at least in theory) of the International Monetary Fund system.

It would be instructive for the reader to analyse the converse case, namely, the international transmission by beggar-my-neighbour policies, not of depression and unemployment, but of *inflation*. It will be found that this can be even more insidious, since the restraints of the risk of unemployment and falling reserves are in this case absent and countries are not under the same pressure to pursue sound international policies. In the 1960s there were complaints by some European economists that their countries were being

90

'infected' through their balance of payments by inflation from the United States. It is curious that economic analysis in general, and the IMF's policies in particular, have paid relatively little attention to what has now become a pressing world problem.

OPEC and the world's money

Following the Middle East War in October 1973 a number of Arab oil-producing countries decided, as part of political pressures aimed at bringing about a settlement of the conflict with Israel, to restrict oil exports to the Western industrialized countries. Out of this action there grew a permanent oil cartel, OPEC, which through its control of oil output was able to raise world oil prices from around $3 per barrel earlier in 1973 to over $10 by late 1975. This development had important effects on the world's money.

(a) *The balance of payments effect.* One effect of dearer oil was to put the industrial countries as a whole in deficit with the oil-producing countries to the tune, initially, of about $60,000 millions annually. In the period that followed, industrial imports by the oil-producing countries did in fact rise substantially, while oil imports by the industrialized countries fell moderately. Even so, the industrialized countries' total 'oil deficit' in 1975 was $35,000 millions and likely to remain large. As a result there were considerable pressures on some of the oil-deficit countries' currencies, notably the pound.

(b) *Financing the oil deficit.* It was necessary to find a method by which those countries with large oil deficits could obtain compensating finance out of the surpluses being earned by the oil exporters. Some finance was provided naturally as oil-producing countries invested in property assets abroad, notably in Britain,[1] France and the United States. In the main, however, oil exporters' surplus revenues accumulated in the form of currency assets, particularly United States dollars deposited in Western and Japanese banks. The problem then arose of re-cycling these petro-dollars to the industrial countries most needing oil finance. The United States scheme was that the oil-producers should agree to deposit petro-dollars in a $25,000 millions fund, either with the OECD or with the Bank for International Settlements, which would then re-cycle the funds as required to industrial member countries. The British scheme was that

---

[1] See Brinley Davies, *Business Finance and the City of London,* Heinemann, 1976, page 64.

the IMF should set up for the use of member countries a $30,000 millions-a-year 'oil facility' by borrowing money at interest directly from the oil-producers. In the event the British scheme was the first to be adopted, in 1975, though the IMF's oil facility was in fact fixed at only $6,000 millions.

(c) *Oil deflation.* Higher oil prices had, from a demand point of view, a deflationary influence on world economic activity, for in effect about 2 per cent (initially) of gross world product was being transferred from industrialized countries' 'spending' to OPEC countries' 'saving'. (It must of course be stressed that dearer oil was *not* the underlying cause of the world recession – or inflation – of the mid-1970s.) As dearer oil added to the industrialized countries' balance of payments difficulties, the risk was increased that some of them might panic into using extensive import restrictions and thereby intensify the world recession. The main aim of the inconclusive Rambouillet 'summit' meeting of six leading industrial countries in November 1975 was to lay the basis for a joint programme to prevent the spread of beggar-my-neighbour policies and facilitate a controlled reflation of the world economy.

(d) *OPEC and international monetary stability.* It was feared in some quarters that the Arab countries might be tempted to use their surplus oil funds to 'rock' the international monetary system, with the aim of persuading the United States and some other Western countries to reduce their support for Israel. In the main however the Arab and other oil-producing countries used their new-found financial power very cautiously. Some of the oil-producers were however worried about accumulating oil funds in the form of weakening reserve currencies – which was why Kuwait, for example, decided in October 1975 to stop accepting crude oil payments in sterling.

Summary

1. The four functions of money greatly assist exchange and specialization both at the national and international level.

2. Economic growth (rising productivity and income per head) takes place partly via new patterns of world specialization and depends partly on international investment flows from developed to less-developed countries.

3. International investment flows can be triggered off by

(*a*) the pressure of demand on raw material resources in developed countries.

(*b*) the pressure of .demand on high-wage labour resources in developed countries.

4. Restrictions on international money payments and international trade damage not only specialization, but the *growth* of specialization.

5. The IMF, the World Bank and GATT were set up after the Second World War to try to ensure an efficient world system of payments, investment and trade.

6. Good-creditor policies and good-debtor policies on the balance of payments facilitate international specialization and economic growth and are more likely to be successfully pursued under a sound international money system.

7. The international transmission of depression or inflation by beggar-my-neighbour policies is less difficult to prevent if there is a stable and flexible international money system.

Appendix to Chapter 8
The international transmission of inflation ('solution' to situation described on page 90).

In essence the sequence of events is parallel to that described on page 89 (the transmission of depression). First, let us take the case of country A which, perhaps because of lax domestic policies, begins to experience inflationary pressure. Suppose that at this stage A still has a strong balance of payments position, and large foreign exchange reserves, together with access to substantial 'second-line' international liquidity; these will greatly reduce the incentive for A to take anti-inflationary measures.

A's inflation will lead to a rise in its imports and a fall in its exports. From the point of view of another country, B, this will mean a rise in exports and fall in imports. This will represent a net injection of expenditure into B's economy and so the level of its income and employment will also tend to increase.

The snag comes if country B is already experiencing full employment: in this event the injection of demand from A will lead to inflationary pressures on B. However B's balance of payments will (until the new income and employment effect have finally worked themselves out) now be stronger than before. So B will be under no great pressure to deal with the inflation imported from A.

The appropriate policy for B and other countries in a similar situation would be to reduce their exports and increase their imports, which would increase the retained output which they have available to absorb their excess demand. This could be done through a higher exchange rate (as in the case of the revaluation of the Swedish crown in 1946); or by reducing import duties and controls; or by levying a tax on exports (for example, Malaya's post-war tax on rubber).

The other element in the international transmission of inflation is the price effect. Primary products are a major import for most industrial countries. Both the demands and the supplies of these products are generally inelastic. So if an inflationary boom takes place in the industrial countries, prices and incomes in the primary producer countries may rise very sharply; this effect will very likely be accentuated by speculative hoarding of primary product stocks by firms and governments in the industrial countries. (As an over-simplification, this may be regarded as an explanation of the world boom in primary product prices in the early 1970s.)

A partial solution to this problem might be – though it would be likely to prove very difficult – a successful international commodity price control policy. This would involve building up large stocks of primary products when the industrial countries' demand for them is slack; and releasing these stocks during a time of boom in the industrial countries when their demand for these products is high.

CASE STUDY 1: THE STERLING CRISIS OF 1964

Theme

Three currency crises in 1964 showed how a currency which is on a fixed exchange rate, and backed by a weak balance of payments, can become a target for speculation. In the worst crisis, that of sterling at the end of the year, ineffective management of Britain's economy was an important factor behind the speculative pressures, which were only overcome by a concerted international rescue operation.

The dollar and the lira

In 1964 pressures on a number of currencies provided a searching test for international monetary co-operation. One currency in trouble was the United States dollar which had been weak for several years because of continued United States balance of payments deficits. As early as March 1961 the dollar had shared in some of the speculative backwash of the Dutch and German currency revaluations, with the result that the United States had taken the step of arranging central bank swap facilities amounting by 1963 to $1,100 millions (later increased to $4,500 millions in 1966). In July 1963, the United States obtained a stand-by credit from the IMF, but early in 1964 speculative pressure on the dollar increased and the United States made its first ever drawing on the IMF – $125 millions, mainly in French and German currency. After this the pressure on the dollar subsided.

A second currency in distress was the Italian lira, following a sharp deterioration in Italy's balance of payments during 1963. Speculative pressure was resisted in mid-March by means of various Basle-type swaps totalling $1,100 millions, plus an IMF drawing of $225 millions. This swift international support led to a sharp fall-off in speculation which stopped altogether later in the year as Italy's balance of payments began to improve.

The weakness of the pound

The third crisis was that of sterling in late 1964. The uncertain management of Britain's economy played a central part in this crisis, which took place against a familiar background of balance of payments weakness arising from inflationary pressures.

Following the 1962 disinflation measures, Britain's economy in 1963 was running below full employment and so the government had decided on a reflationary policy. The 1963 Budget reduced taxes by £270 millions and bank advances also rose, by about one-seventh. Output increased rapidly but by 1964 the output ceiling of extreme full employment was being encountered and, with the continuing growth of demand, costs and prices began to rise. As the 1964 monthly trade figures were published there was increasing evidence that Britain's balance of payments was running into substantial deficit. Yet little disinflationary action was taken, apart from raising the duties on alcohol and tobacco by £100 millions in the 1964 budget. Why was this? There seem to have been two reasons. First, the rapid rise in production was causing a sharp fall in manufacturers' stocks of fuel and raw materials; as these stocks were replaced, it was inevitable that imports would for a time rise briskly. After this point however imports should slow down. (Later analysis of the import statistics bears this out.) Secondly, it was hoped that a rapid growth of production would reduce Britain's unit costs and so make its products more competitive in the longer run. This view was associated with official optimism that Britain's economy was now, due to economic planning and the fruits of past investments, physically capable of economic growth of perhaps 4 per cent annually.

It is this second point which has been disputed. By late 1964 unemployment was already down to 1·5 per cent of the labour force, and there was, even allowing for some possible addition to the labour force (for example more married women), little hope therefore for any permanent large growth of output. Due to labour shortages, wages were now advancing at about 8 per cent a year. Nowadays this rate of increase appears attractively low, but compared with Britain's competitors at that time it was dangerously high. It has been doubted therefore whether Britain's exports could have increased very much in the short and medium term as a result of the 1964 'dash for freedom'. If devaluation had been included as a possibility in the mix of policy alternatives, the chances of a successful home-based expansion leading to greater efficiency and high exports might have been much better, but the government apparently ruled devaluation out.

As the bad trade figures continued, speculative pressure on the pound built up steadily and the sensational developments which followed the general election obscured for the time being the question of the long-term trend of Britain's balance of payments.

SUMMARY OF 1964 BALANCE OF PAYMENTS

Current Account	£ millions
Visible trade	— 519
Invisibles	+ 124
Current balance	— 395
Currency flows	
Current balance	— 395
Capital flows	— 289
Balancing item	— 11
Total currency flow	— 695
Official financing	
Official borrowing	+ 573
Decrease in reserves	+ 122
Total	+ 695

The sterling crisis breaks

After the October election the new Labour government expressed its surprise at how bad the official balance of payments figures actually were: the current account deficit was being estimated at about £400 millions for the whole year, and the long-term capital outflow was also thought to be running at about £400 millions (giving a negative total currency flow of £800 millions). Actually it was a mistake for the government to dramatize, for domestic political reasons, the seriousness of the balance of payments problem, for this made the position of the pound weaker than ever. As far as policy measures were concerned the government began by considering devaluing the pound as a way of improving the balance of payments and reversing speculation. However it quickly rejected this. Perhaps it was influenced by the fact that it had been Labour politicians who had devalued the pound both in 1931 and in 1949. The latter devaluation was much criticized as excessive, or even harmful, in view of the fact that Britain's import and export elasticities of demand were low after the Second World War.

At the same time, however, the new government's ministers

97

decided against orthodox fiscal and monetary methods of reducing inflationary pressures – probably because, before the election, when in opposition, they had forcefully criticized the Conservative government's 'stop-go' policies. In effect, therefore, the new government, largely because of its own statements and attitudes, found it had sacrificed both of the two basic types of policy for dealing with a balance of payments deficit, namely, the external one (changing the exchange rate) and the internal one (disinflating domestic demand). It is not surprising that it rapidly found itself pushed from one makeshift measure to another, as the speculative pressures on the pound got worse and worse.

From pillar to post
First, only ten days after the election, it announced a temporary 15 per cent import surcharge (that is, tariff) on imports of manufactured goods. This was a bad mistake. It was a blatant beggar-my-neighbour measure which violated the GATT agreement, and antagonized foreign governments, businessmen and consumers. In any case, it had only a limited effect on the volume of imports because many firms exporting to Britain, knowing the surcharge was to be temporary, trimmed their profits and held on to their markets. Moreover, the extreme haste of the tariff announcement increased nervousness abroad about the weakness of the pound. (The surcharge was reduced to 10 per cent in April 1965, and finally ceased in November 1966.)

The second measure was a November budget and this too turned out to be a mistake. By merely hinting at possible future tax increases and doing little to tackle existing inflation, it was psychologically a bad anticlimax. Speculative pressure on the pound continued. In an important speech the Prime Minister stressed that the pound would be defended 'whatever the cost'. When in the days following this speech no new measures were announced, the pressure on the reserves became worse than ever. Devaluation rumours were now in the air.

The third measure was unexpected: it was an increase in Bank Rate from 5 per cent to 7 per cent, *on a Monday*. This unusual measure quickly turned speculation against the pound into an avalanche.

The fourth measure, arranged literally at the last minute over the telephone by the Governor of the Bank of England, was the creation of a line of foreign exchange credit to help defend the pound. Already a number of Basle-type swaps amounting to $500 millions had had to be activated to counter speculation. What the Governor now arranged was a swap between the Bank of England and eleven other central banks, totalling $3,000 millions. This massive defence line finally stopped speculation dead in its tracks. A further support, obtained in early December, was an IMF stand-by credit of $1,000 millions, partly activated under the General Arrangements to Borrow, which enabled the central bank swaps to be repaid in May 1965.

However there still remained the problem of longer term measures to improve Britain's balance of payments. Unless the breathing space purchased by the international loans was wisely used a new sterling crisis would certainly develop sooner or later.

Postscript
In fact the opportunity was not taken. Inflation and over-full employment were allowed to continue in Britain through 1965 and 1966. The balance of payments remained weak and the pound had to be supported on a number of occasions against speculation. Although the balance of payments seemed to be improving for a while early in 1967, new pressures on the balance of payments led to a further crisis which culminated in the 1967 devaluation of the pound (Case Study 2).

CASE STUDY 2: INTERNATIONAL ASPECTS OF THE 1967 STERLING DEVALUATION

Theme
The 1967 devaluation of the pound is a good case study of a technically successful devaluation operation involving a key world currency. There are two aspects which are worth examining. The first is the significance of Britain's sterling balance liabilities, which greatly increased the vulnerability of the pound to speculation both before and after devaluation and which necessitated international support for the pound in the form of the 1968 Basle arrangements. The second aspect is the extensive and confidential discussions which took place between Britain and the other countries to determine a degree of sterling devaluation which would be sufficient to help restore Britain's balance of payments but not so large as to provoke retaliatory devaluations.

Background
The decision to devalue the pound in November 1967 took place against a background of persistent balance of payments weakness

BALANCE OF PAYMENTS SUMMARY 1964 TO 1968[1]

	£ millions	
Currency flows		
Current balance	− 900	
Long-term capital flows	− 900	
Short-term capital flows	− 1800	
Total currency flow		− 3600
Official financing		
Net IMF drawings	+ 1100	
Central bank borrowings	+ 2000	
Decrease in reserves[2]	+ 500	
Total official financing		+ 3600

[1] From S. Brittan, *Steering the Economy*, Penguin 1971, p. 390.
[2] Including sale of Treasury dollar portfolio.

100

arising mainly from the failure of successive British governments to overcome inflation.

Throughout much of 1964, 1965, and 1966, monetary demand was ahead of production, and, due to rapidly rising costs and prices, British products were becoming less competitive, and less profitable, on world markets. In spite of the incomes freeze of mid-1966 Britain's balance of payments remained weak, although at one time early in 1967 it seemed for a while to be improving.

Even without the balance of payments figures, the weakness of the pound could be deduced from the amount of support it needed in the three years up to the 1967 devaluation. International facilities made available in this period to the Bank of England included: a $1,000 million line of credit with various central banks; a swap arrangement of $1,350 millions with the United States Federal Reserve Bank; a loan of about $100 millions from some Swiss commercial banks; and a special short-term credit from central banks of $250 millions.

The build-up of the crisis

In the early months of 1967 there was mounting evidence that Britain's balance of payments was moving further into the red. In the first half of the year there was a current account deficit of about £100 millions, and this was followed in the second half by a deficit of about £400 millions, giving a current account deficit for the whole year of approximately £500 millions. At first, there was an inflow of short-term capital which offset the pressure on the current account. But in the third quarter of the year capital started to leave Britain as speculative selling of sterling developed. Apart from the underlying factor of inflation other causes of Britain's widening payments gap were: the slow-down in British exports due to recessions in the United States and German markets; the rather higher volume of imports after the lifting of the last stage of the 1964 import surcharge; the closing of the Suez Canal during the Middle East War which increased the cost of Britain's imports; and the London and Liverpool dock strikes which reduced Britain's exports more than its imports. Lastly, there were doubts connected with Britain's second application to join the Common Market; it was widely believed that if Britain entered the market a devaluation of the pound would be necessary to offset the estimated short-run balance of payments burden of between £450 millions and £900 millions which would

101

result from its EEC obligations. Most of these factors were temporary, but combined with the underlying weakness of sterling, their overall effect was to break the back of the pound. In spite of the doubtful balance of payments situation, the government introduced in the middle of 1967 a number of reflationary measures intended to reduce unemployment, which had risen since the deflationary measures taken in 1966.

In June 1967, hire purchase regulations were relaxed and future increases of pensions and family allowances announced, followed, at the end of August, by a further easing of hire purchase conditions. Meanwhile, speculative pressures on the pound continued.

With the worsening balance of payments situation it became evident to the government that there were only two basic courses of action open: it must either obtain a really large foreign loan to support Britain's foreign exchange reserves, while long-term measures were taken to improve the balance of payments; or it must be prepared to accept a devaluation of the pound (contingency plans for which were already in existence at the Treasury).

The sterling balances

The existence of large British sterling balance liabilities abroad affected the circumstances of the 1967 devaluation of the pound in a number of ways. An important element in the balances reflected sterling's role as a reserve currency held by the sterling area countries. Potentially this was a source of substantial speculative pressure as had been shown ten years earlier, after the 1956 Middle East War, when sales of sterling made necessary an IMF rescue operation for the pound. In practice, though, these balances were generally stable partly because of their usefulness as reserve currency, and partly no

BRITAIN'S STERLING LIABILITIES 1963 TO 1968

Year	Sterling balance liabilities	IMF and central bank liabilities	Total
		£ millions	
1963	3262	627	3889
1964	3305	991	4296
1965	3375	1481	4856
1966	3494	1655	5149
1967	3806	1540	5346
1968	3950	2082	6032

doubt because of the relatively high rate of interest which the British government paid on them. They were not, therefore, an important factor in the build-up of speculation before the devaluation of the pound.

An argument which was sometimes used against devaluing the pound was that it would be a breach of trust with the rest of the Sterling Area, since the value of its sterling reserves would automatically be reduced. Whether this was a sound argument is debatable: the effects of a possible devaluation of the pound were presumably reflected in, and offset by, the high rate of interest paid to holders of sterling balances by the British government. Nevertheless the argument seems to have influenced British governments in the 1960s.[1] It is interesting to note, moreover, that some of the Sterling Area governments appear to have been genuinely surprised at the devaluation of the pound when it finally came.

The other main element in the sterling balances reflected the pound's role as a world trading currency. Unlike the Sterling Area balances these short-term trading balances were not at all stable. As doubts developed in 1967 about the future of the pound, substantial amounts of these funds were rapidly withdrawn from London – possibly as much as £200 millions in the final days of the crisis.

The mechanics of exchange rate consultation

Early in November 1967 the British government received fresh economic forecasts pointing to a continuing balance of payments deficit for 1968. On 16 November the Cabinet, against a background of massive speculation against sterling, took the decision (in secret) to devalue the pound.

How much any particular country with a serious balance of payments deficit needs to devalue its currency by, is never an easy question to decide. As we saw earlier, the effects depend not only on the elasticities of demand for imports and exports (covering thousands of different goods and services) but also on the scope for increased exports and import-substitution. In November 1967 a sterling devaluation of about 15 per cent was being informally mooted abroad by British representatives.

Apparently there were difficulties.[2] One was the attitude of the

---

[1] S. Brittan, *op. cit.*, p. 447.

[2] S. Brittan, *op. cit.*, p. 360.

French, who seemed to be against the idea of a sterling devaluation and would not say whether the franc would follow a devalued pound downwards. Another was the attitude of the United States which was worried about the dollar and would have preferred international support action to maintain the $2·80 sterling parity, together with the existing world alignment of exchange rates. On the evening of 17 November, the British government however took the step of informing the IMF's managing director about its decision to devalue the pound. The United States President was also informed at this time. On 18 November the par value of the pound was officially lowered from 2·48828 to 2·13281 grams of gold, that is, from $2·80 to $2·40, representing a sterling devaluation of 14·3 per cent. The exchange rate limits for the pound now became $2·38 to $2·42.

Technically, the devaluation of the pound turned out to be a highly successful operation. Due to the extensive information negotiations preceding it, few countries followed the devalued pound; moreover, a substantial additional amount of international credit was obtained to support the pound during the post-devaluation period. Even in the Sterling Area, whose members traditionally maintained fixed exchange rates against the pound, only a few countries followed Britain's move, notably New Zealand and Eire. The other main country to devalue was Denmark. As the devaluing countries were, in most instances, suppliers of Britain's basic imports such as foodstuffs, their action probably did more good than harm to Britain's trading position. The great industrial countries against which Britain was trying to improve its competitive position – the United States, Germany, Japan, France, Italy and the Low Countries – did not devalue.

CURRENCIES WHICH FOLLOWED STERLING IN 1967

Currency		New exchange rate against sterling	Percentage devaluation
New Zealand	dollar	2·143	19·45
Ceylon	rupee	14·288	20·00
Hong Kong	dollar	14·545	5·70
Irish Republic	pound	1·000	14·29
Denmark	crown	18·000	7·90
Spain	peseta	168·000	14·29
Israel	pound	8·400	14·29
Brazil	cruz.	7·700	15·70

According to the Bank of England's quarterly bulletin, the understanding with which the devaluation had been accepted without widespread devaluations of other important currencies was an outstanding feature of the operation. It certainly contrasts with the 1949 sterling devaluation, when almost all the West European currencies followed the pound to a lower exchange rate. For this reason, the 14 per cent devaluation of sterling in 1967 was probably effectively greater than the 30 per cent devaluation in 1949!

The Letter of Intent

To support the effects of the devaluation on Britain's balance of payments position, the government negotiated an immediate stand-by credit of $1,400 millions at the IMF. In addition, a number of foreign central banks agreed to provide a further $1,500 millions of support facilities for the pound. A Letter of Intent which accompanied the request for IMF help set out the policies which the British government intended to use to strengthen the balance of payments by at least £500 millions a year – which was expected to lead to a current account surplus of £100 million in the second half of 1968. The basic policy was to be one of disinflation of domestic demand by about £800 millions *below what would otherwise have been the case*. In other words, there would be a cut-back, *but not a reduction*. The IMF was also to be consulted if further disinflationary measures proved necessary. The measures taken would be both fiscal (a slow-down in government spending, particularly on military bases abroad) and monetary (dearer and tighter credit measures accompanied the devaluation announcement). A tightening of the existing prices and incomes policy also took place.

In the March 1968 budget the government increased indirect taxes by £800 millions which, it was estimated, would release about £500 millions of resources for exports and import substitution.

The pound in trouble

However the hoped-for improvement in the strength of the pound after devaluation did not occur; there was no quick reversal of speculation and no rapid recovery in Britain's reserves. An important reason for this was the belief of holders of sterling that the British government was not really prepared to disinflate domestic spending sufficiently to release all the resources needed for increased exports and import substitution. As early as December 1967 there was selling of sterling on the foreign exchange market in anticipation of a possible second devaluation of the pound. The speculative pressures continued into 1968 when they were particularly severe at the time of the French student troubles in May and again during the European currency crisis in November.

One factor behind the speculation was the fact that a number of Sterling Area countries had been taken by surprise by the sterling devaluation, and were now, with rumours of a possible second devaluation, diversifying their reserves by selling pounds (to the extent of about £280 millions) and buying other reserve assets. Also for a time in late November and December 1967, the pressure on sterling was, we are told,[1] 'aggravated by a French war of nerves primarily designed against the dollar but which did not hesitate to use sterling as an instrument; and rumours about difficulties in negotiating the IMF credit for the pound flowed out thick and fast from 'Paris'. Another factor was the backwash from speculative purchases of gold, which took the form of sales of reserve currencies like the dollar and sterling. (This was itself partly a feed-back effect from the sterling devaluation which had undermined confidence in the reserve currencies.)

The Basle Group arrangements of 1966 and 1968

The devaluation of sterling led to a loss in the value of the sterling reserves of overseas countries, whether or not they devalued their currencies alongside the pound. In the early part of 1968 central banks in the Sterling Area were selling sterling reserves and it became necessary for Britain to find international support to offset and, if possible, arrest the run-down in the sterling balances. Already in 1966 at an agreement in Basle a number of central banks had made available to Britain a credit for this purpose. In September 1968 this arrangement was enlarged and made more formal.[2] First, twelve central banks undertook to make available to Britain through the Bank for International Settlement, credits worth $2000 millions on which the Bank of England could draw over the next three years, to finance any running down of the Sterling Area balances; drawings were to be repaid within ten years. This support made it possible for Britain to negotiate undertakings from the governments of the rest

---

[1] S. Brittan, *op. cit.*, p. 378.

[2] 'The Evolution of the Sterling Area', *MBR*, February 1967.

of the Sterling Area to maintain agreed proportions of their foreign reserves in sterling, based on the position at the middle of 1968. For example, in the case of Australia, the proportion was 40 per cent. In return Britain gave guarantees, in terms of the United States dollar, which effectively safeguarded for a period of three years 90 per cent of the sterling balances against any loss which might arise in the event of a future devaluation of the pound. At the same time, it was announced that the earlier 1966 Basle facility, which related to fluctuations in all overseas countries' sterling balances, would be gradually wound up. In 1971 most of the three-year agreements, together with the Basle facility, were renewed.

Postscript

The 1967 devaluation of the pound paid off – but it was a long haul, and progress was much slower than expected. Britain's exports responded well to the lower exchange rate, increasing in 1968 by 14 per cent in terms of volume, and 23 per cent in terms of value. Imports on the other hand also rose in volume, by 11 per cent – 22 per cent in value. The current account therefore remained in deficit in 1968. It was not until 1969 that the break-through came in the shape of a current account surplus, which became substantial in 1970 and 1971.

By then Britain had started to face a new problem, unemployment, which was a result of the prolonged deflationary measures which had followed the 1967 devaluation. To help increase employment the government (by now a Conservative one again) adopted a reflationary programme, based on heavy budget deficit financing together with a rapidly expanding money supply. This certainly did the trick, for by 1972 the growth in production and demand was such that widespread labour shortages were developing. Unfortunately, and predictably, it was at the cost of renewed inflation. In a short time, Britain's balance of payments was moving back into deficit. It was not long before the next sterling crisis was on the way, culminating in the decision of June 1972 to float the pound (Case Study 3).

107

CASE STUDY 3: STERLING AND THE 1973 INTERNATIONAL MONETARY CRISIS

Theme
In 1973 the world's two reserve main currencies, the dollar and the pound, each of which was backed by a weak balance of payments, came under severe speculative pressures. International monetary instability was made worse by the effects of the EEC system of jointly-fixed exchange rates known as the 'snake in the tunnel',[1] which offered tempting one-way options to speculators.

The weakness of the pound
We saw earlier that the basic factor behind the government's decision in 1972 to float the pound out of the EEC 'snake' was inflation, which continued to weaken Britain's balance of payments. We saw, too, that at times the rate of exchange of the floating pound was driven down by speculative pressures, which weakened its balance of payments even further.

Matters came to a head in the summer of 1973 when the pound began to depreciate steeply on the foreign exchange markets. At the end of May, the foreign exchange value of the pound was already about 10 per cent below that of early 1972. In September, when at one point the pound depreciated by 3 per cent in three days, it had fallen by over 18 per cent, and in January 1974 it reached a record low of only $2·20, representing a depreciation against foreign currencies in general of one-fifth in two years.

The J-curve effect
The unnaturally low exchange rate of sterling in 1973 might have been expected, by increasing the volume of Britain's exports and reducing that of imports, to lead in the longer run to a very strong balance of payments position. In the short run, however, when the scope for changes in the import and export volumes was very limited, the effect of the low sterling exchange rate was to increase the sterling payments for imports and reduce the earning value of exports – which proved very damaging to Britain's balance of payments. These

---

[1] p. 67.

opposing results, over a period of time, of a low exchange rate, are sometimes described as the J-curve effect.[1] In the latter part of 1973 a yawning monthly trade gap of £300 millions opened up. For the whole of 1973 Britain's deficit on trade was £2,400 millions, while the deficit on the current account was £1,400 millions. Also, the increase in the sterling price of Britain's imports which was caused by the hefty depreciation of the pound, and reinforced by the world-wide boom in commodity prices at that time, accelerated the rise in the cost of living in 1973. The effect was to undermine the government's prices and incomes policy and make the prospects for the pound bleaker still. In an attempt to deal with the situation, it was decided to introduce a tighter monetary policy.

In July 1973 the Bank of England called for a total of 4 per cent of special deposits from the banking sector. The Bank of England's minimum lending rate also rose, reaching a record 13 per cent by November. Unfortunately, an increased foreign demand for sterling did not materialize and the pound continued to weaken. Also, higher interest rates worked against the government's programme for containing wage cost inflation.

The international speculation problem

An important factor behind international currency speculation in 1973 was the working of the EEC 'snake in the tunnel' system of jointly fixed exchange rates. The idea was that coordinated policies among the EEC countries aimed at stabilizing their relative cost and price levels, would allow their currencies' exchange rates to be tied within close limits. In fact, however, the divergent pressures on individual 'snake' currencies proved considerable, and tempting one-way options were set up for speculators resulting in pressures which affected the dollar, and even the floating pound, which by 1973 was in no way directly connected with the 'snake'.

At first the selling pressure was mainly on the United States dollar. In February 1973 when the United States trade deficit of $6,000 millions for 1972 was published, speculators started to sell dollars and buy stronger currencies, particularly the German mark, which they were hoping to force through the ceiling of the 'snake'. Between 6 and 9 February 1973 support purchases cost the German central bank $4,000 millions. At this point, international talks were held and

---

[1] p. 61.

led to most of the 'snake' currencies, including the mark, being up-valued by 10 per cent against the dollar. The speculators had won a handsome victory! About this time Japan, Switzerland and Italy, to deter speculative pressures, decided to float their currencies.

In March 1973 the battle was joined again between the speculators and the central banks. This time the foreign exchange markets were

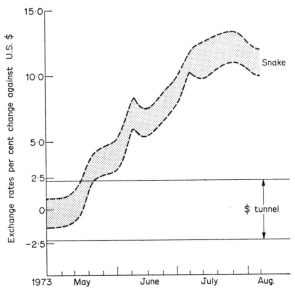

Figure 11.1   The 'snake' leaves the 'tunnel'

closed for a whole week to allow international consultations. When the markets opened, the German mark had been revalued yet again – this time by three per cent against the other 'snake' currencies. Another win for the speculators! At least, however, there was one gain from the episode – namely, the decision of the EEC countries to abandon the 'tunnel', that is, their fixed exchange rates against the dollar. This meant that from now on, the 'snake' currencies, and the dollar, would float against one another, and the options for speculation would thus be reduced.

The international position, then, at the middle of 1973 was that several mutually floating currency groups had emerged: the pound sterling; the United States dollar; the Japanese yen; the EEC 'snake currencies'; and various other currencies such as the Swiss franc and the Italian lira. It is important to note that much of the floating was 'dirty'. In other words, the central banks, including the Bank of England, were to a degree holding their exchange rates artificially, by means of substantial foreign exchange intervention, together, in many cases, with extensive exchange controls.

The pound and the 'snake'

For most of this period the floating pound had not been greatly affected by speculative movements. However, in June 1973 Britain's poor balance of trade figures, which were partly associated with the continuing failure of the government to contain inflation, led to the pound following the dollar down. Towards the end of the month a very tight monetary policy in West Germany attracted speculative funds there, and on 29 June the speculators won yet again – this time the mark was upvalued by $5\frac{1}{2}$ per cent. Even so, by late July, speculative buying was again threatening to push the mark out of the top of the 'snake'. As *The Economist* newspaper frequently pointed out at the time,[1] speculators were dumping dollars and pounds on to the German central bank, knowing that the Bundesbank's commitment to keep the German mark within the EEC 'snake' obliged it to buy foreign exchange at a time when a depreciation of the dollar and the pound was clearly imminent. As long as the German mark remained in the 'snake', speculators knew what currencies to buy and sell.

These international monetary difficulties continued into 1974, and were aggravated both by the international gold-buying rush (Case Study 4) and by the economic effects of sharp increase in world prices, which put the balance of payments of most of the industrial countries into substantial deficit. It was against this background that the French franc began to come under heavy speculative pressures. The result was that the French government, in January 1974, took the decision to float the franc – an action which dealt a severe blow to (what was left of) the EEC 'snake'. A hopeful note, however, was the strengthening of the dollar as the United States seemed at last to be moving into a position of balance of payments strength, particularly now that the oil crisis had revealed its relatively strong energy position.

---

[1] For example see *The Economist*, July 14, 1973, p. 11.

Euro-currencies

An additional factor making for instability in recent years was the activities of the Euro-dollar market, which had become a very important medium of private and semi-official international liquidity, and thus of potential speculative pressures. By 1971 the quantity of funds in the Euro-dollar market was half as large as the total of all countries' foreign exchange reserves, plus the entire IMF currency pool! Euro-dollars are United States dollars which have been deposited with banks outside the United States. In a sense they are dollars which have lost their way and started a new life overseas. The origins of the market go back to the period after 1945 when holders of dollar balances in the communist bloc placed them with London banks who then re-lent them elsewhere in Europe. Then, in the 1950s and 1960s, the United States payments deficit led to a massive outflow of dollars to other countries, part of this 'overhang' being held in the form of central banks' reserves and part as Euro-dollar deposits.

The period of the dollar credits varies from a few days up to ten or more years and the market until recently was dominated by the British banks. The main use of Euro-dollars is to finance international trade, but longer-term loans are used to finance foreign investments (for example large foreign borrowings by Britain's nationalized industries in 1973).[1]

An important reason for the rapid growth of the Euro-dollar market was the fact that rates of interest in the United States, and therefore on Euro-dollar credits, were often relatively low, thus making Euro-dollars an attractive form of borrowing. Also the Euro-dollar business can be run on small margins since credits in the market are limited to large amounts, usually $1 million or more. The expansion of the market has been augmented by the growth of a 'credit pyramid' of Euro-dollars similar to that inside an ordinary domestic banking system. From about 1970 there was also a growing market in Euro-sterling, Euro-marks and other national currencies and the area of the Euro-markets had by now extended to the Middle East, Australia, Japan and other countries. Thus, in the uncertain conditions of 1973 the scope for short-term capital movements based on Euro-currency transactions, was very considerable.

---

[1] p. 29.

As an example, early in 1974 the French government – like many others – was faced with a large oil-deficit on the balance of payments. It decided to finance this by raising large loans on the Euro-dollar market. This was associated with large French sales of dollars, which contributed to the depreciation of that currency at that time.

The floating pound in the mid-1970s

We saw earlier that in 1973 the pound depreciated considerably, against a background of balance of payments deficit associated with rapid domestic inflation and rising world commodity prices. These difficulties continued in 1974 and were exacerbated by the steep rise in oil import costs due to OPEC oil policies (see page 91). In 1975 Britain had a current account deficit of £1,700 millions (after a record deficit of £3,800 in 1974). In the last quarter of 1974 sterling weakened sharply and speculation intensified when Saudi Arabia decided to protect itself against further exchange losses by ceasing to accept oil receipts in sterling. The Bank of England's reserves now fell sharply as it supported the pound.

Speculation against sterling continued in 1975 and by June of that year the pound had depreciated by 29 per cent against its 1972 'Smithsonian' value. The obvious inability of the British government to reduce the current level of inflation led to fresh fears about the future of sterling and in October 1975 Kuwait decided to stop accepting sterling for oil payments. In spite of some reduced imports, due to fuel economies and the domestic recession, Britain's 1975 current account deficit was about £2,000 millions. In November 1975 Britain informed the IMF that it wished to apply for a first tranche[1] of £400 millions together with a drawing of £575 millions on the IMF's new 'oil facility' (see page 92).

The medium- and long-term prospects for Britain's balance of payments, and for sterling, in the remainder of the 1970s seemed to depend on three main factors: a hoped-for expansion of inter-national trade, and hence British export prospects, if and when the world recession came to an end; a successful control of domestic inflation so that Britain's exporters could take advantage of any world trade up-swing; and the substantial import savings expected from the late 1970s when North Sea oil came into full flow.

---

[1] See page 41.

CASE STUDY 4: THE 1973-74 GOLD-BUYING BOOM

Theme

The 1973 gold-buying rush, which contributed to the problems of the dollar and the pound, was connected with the United States policy of pegging, at an artificially low level, the 'official' price of gold bought and sold between central banks.[1] The likelihood that this policy would sooner or later fail, and the official price of gold be increased in line with that of the free market, led in the end to heavy speculative sales of dollars and other weak currencies.

Background to the crisis

Unless central banks co-operate closely, and manage their respective currencies skilfully, on the basis of really large foreign exchange reserves, any fixed exchange rate system is very prone to speculative pressures. We saw earlier how this was a factor in the difficulties of the pound in 1964 and in 1967; and how in 1973, when a number of currencies were floating, the EEC 'snake in the tunnel' system of jointly-fixed exchange rates led to heavy speculative buying of German marks and sales of dollars and pounds.

A 'fixed rate element' which for a number of years provided good opportunities for speculators was the long-standing policy of the United States of keeping the official world price of gold fixed in terms of the dollar. It led eventually to the gold-dollar crisis of 1973, which in turn adversely affected Britain in a number of ways. First, the flight out of weaker currencies into gold was one factor behind the unhealthy depreciation of the pound. Secondly, general speculative pressures intensified the increase in world primary product prices which Britain, along with other industrial countries, found a heavy import burden. And thirdly, speculative movements out of securities into gold (and shares in gold-mining companies) were one factor behind the fall in stock-market values which unsettled business confidence in Britain and in other countries.

Until about 1960 the United States gold reserve was so large that

---

[1] p. 50.

it could successfully keep the world price of gold pegged at $35 an ounce. Later, due to balance of payments difficulties, the United States gold reserve became insufficient for it to continue to do this alone. A central bank gold pool of $80 millions was therefore set up, in 1962, with which it proved possible for a number of years to supply the world's markets with sufficient gold to absorb any speculative buying based on expectations that the gold price might eventually be increased.

Gold speculation begins

In 1968, however, the central banks found it increasingly difficult to absorb further speculative gold sales, and a 'two-tier' scheme was introduced. The central banks' cartel continued to fix the price at $35 in the official sector; but the price of gold on the private market was now freed from central bank intervention and left to the forces of supply and demand. This was the thin end of the wedge for speculators, for the higher the free market gold price became, the more likely it was that the official price would, sooner or later, have to be increased. Moreover, the longer this move was delayed, the greater would be the tendency for newly-mined gold to be sold on the profitable private market and for central bank gold to be sold, by legal and illegal means, into private hands. Thus, the central banks' ability to fix an official price would diminish even further.

The 1971 dollar crisis, which led the United States government to suspend the official convertibility of dollars into gold at central bank level, weakened the official gold market still further. While in December of that year the Smithsonian Agreement raised the price of gold, in terms of the (inconvertible) United States dollar, to $38.

By now it was looking as if there might quite soon be a really substantial devaluation of the dollar in terms of gold, and speculators started to find methods, often very indirect ones, to buy gold on a large scale.

The peak of gold speculation

In the summer of 1972 there was considerable uncertainty about the future of the dollar, and the free market price of gold rose from $50, in May, to $70 in August. However reports that Russia would be needing to sell gold to western countries to finance its imports of wheat, led to some speculative selling of gold, and the price settled around $65. But in February 1973, when the United States balance

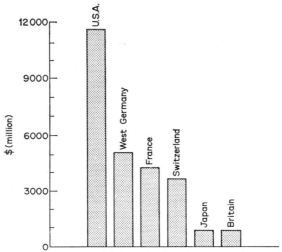

Figure 12.1   Gold reserves 1973 (valued at $38 per oz.)

of payments and the dollar remained weak, new international monetary instabilities set in, as a result of which a second devaluation of the dollar took place against other currencies, the central bank price of gold now being raised to $42. This merely whetted the appetites of the speculators, who continued to sell the weaker currencies and buy gold: in the spring of 1973 the free market gold price reached $91, and in May it touched $111. The main backwash was hitting the dollar, but by now the pound was also being depressed. The continuing Watergate affair led to a further wave of speculative dollar sales, with gold reaching $127 in early June. After this there were signs that the United States balance of payments was starting to improve and some speculators began to buy back the dollar, which now improved both against other currencies and in terms of gold, the price of which fell to around $95.

In November 1973 United States government statements indicated it might at last be ready to abandon the two-tier gold system and agree to the central banks being free to sell and buy gold at market prices.

Early in 1974, however, fears about accelerating inflation in the industrialized countries led to renewed heavy buying of gold and the other precious metals. In February 1974 the free market price of

116

gold on the London and Zurich bullion markets reached $163, representing an increase of 40 per cent in seven weeks!

The lessons of the 1973–74 gold crisis

There are at least two ways in which the 1973 gold buying boom could have been lessened or even prevented.[1] One would have been for the United States Federal Reserve Bank, supported by the other central banks, to have stated at an early stage that it would be prepared to unload its entire gold reserve of over 13,000 tons on to the free market at any price over, say, $150. The other method would have been for the United States and the other central banks to have agreed to support gold at, say, $150 by buying and selling gold on the open market at that price. Either policy would have ruled out any further increase in the world price of gold for years to come and would almost certainly have put a quick end to speculation. (It might also, as we saw earlier,[2] have allowed the United States to pay off its dollar balance debts abroad.)

The moral of the 1973–74 gold story is that the international monetary system cannot be broken up into water-tight compartments. Fixed rate rigidities of whatever kind – adjustable pegs, 'snakes', fixed gold prices – inevitably invite speculative instabilities which quickly spill over from one area into others. There would seem therefore to be fundamentally two choices of policy in international monetary matters. The first is for the world's monetary authorities to go for a fixed exchange rate system, and underpin it by co-operating to control and stabilize all the areas of international monetary activity. The second choice is to opt for floating exchange rates by establishing genuinely free conditions in all forms of markets for foreign exchange. It seems unlikely that any in-between policy has much chance of succeeding.

Falling gold prices in 1975

In 1974 the demand for gold remained high and in December of that year the market price reached $190. Two bull points for gold speculators at this time were the continuing weakness of the United States dollar and the United States advance decision to allow its residents to hold gold from January 1975. In the event, when 2 million ounces

---

[1] *The Economist*, May 19, 1973, p. 88.

[2] p. 75.

of gold were auctioned from the United States Treasury's reserves, there was little buying from investors and the market price of gold quickly fell to $170. For much of 1975 gold markets remained quiet, though there were spells of selling which tended to depress the market price.

It was decided in principle at the August 1975 meeting of the IMF (and confirmed in January 1976) to allow that institution to sell off some of its gold holdings. This announcement led to some speculative selling of gold and prices fell further. In spite of French objections to this policy, all the signs now seemed to point to a continuing reduction in the international role of gold, with periodic sales of IMF gold both to central banks and, indirectly at least, to the free markets. Moreover, during 1975 the United States balance of payments, and hence the dollar, were becoming much stronger, and this further weakened the case for speculative gold buying. At the close of 1975 the gold price was down to $141. Unless renewed world inflation provoked a resumption of the speculative demand for gold, it seemed unlikely that there would be any repeat of the frenzied gold-buying boom of 1973 and 1974.

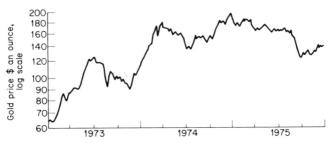

Figure 12.2   Gold prices, 1973–75.

QUESTIONS

1. In what circumstances might a country devalue its currency? (LONDON)
2. What is the problem of international liquidity? Discuss alternative means of dealing with it. (LONDON)
3. Discuss the merits and demerits of floating exchange rates in the light of the experience of recent years. (LONDON)
4. What do you understand by the term 'flexible exchange rates'? What are the disadvantages of flexible exchange rates? Can these disadvantages be overcome by fixed exchange rates? (LONDON)
5. 'Devaluation worsens the terms of trade and is therefore harmful.' Discuss. (LONDON)
6. Evaluate the role of the International Monetary Fund in the post-1945 world economy. (LONDON)
7. Would a floating exchange rate help to remedy an adverse Balance of Payments? (LONDON)
8. If the balance of payments must always balance, why do governments worry about balance of payments deficits? (CAMBRIDGE)
9. (a) In what sense may a currency be undervalued?
   (b) What are the measures necessary to maintain an undervalued rate of exchange?
   (c) What are the likely economic consequences of such an undervaluation? (CAMBRIDGE)
10. 'Devaluation may be necessary to overcome a fundamental disequilibrium in a country's balance of payments, but it is rarely sufficient in itself.' Discuss in the light of British experience since 1967. (CAMBRIDGE)
11. (a) In what sense may the currency of a country be overvalued?
    (b) What are the likely effects of overvaluation?
    (c) What may be done to correct the overvaluation? (CAMBRIDGE)
12. How may alterations in a country's foreign exchange rate affect its foreign exchange reserves? (CAMBRIDGE)
13. Outline the case for and against allowing the value of sterling

on the Foreign Exchange Market to be determined by the forces of the market. (AEB)

14. Estimate the effect of Special Drawing Rights on the development of international trade. (AEB)

15. Critically assess the efficiency of gold as the basis of a country's currency. (AEB)

16. How may a balance of payments deficit be financed?

17. To what extent are deflation and devaluation alternative methods of correcting a balance of payments deficit?

18. 'If deficit countries mended their ways there would be no international monetary problem.' How true was this:
    (a) in the 1960s
    (b) in the early 1970s?

19. Why was it thought necessary to introduce Special Drawing Rights? How successfully have they worked?

20. Should the International Monetary Fund have the powers of a world central bank?

21. What factors lay behind Britain's decision to float the pound in 1972? How successful was the experiment?

22. 'The operation of the EEC snake-in-the-tunnel exchange rate scheme was harmful not only for the fixed-rate currencies but also for the floating currencies.' How true is this?

23. 'There is only one fundamental international monetary problem – speculation.' Comment.

24. Why did Britain run into balance of payments difficulties in 1973?

25. In what sense did the gold standard have 'an inherently deflationary bias'?

26. 'A gold exchange standard has all the vices and none of the virtues of a full gold standard.' Comment.

27. 'If one trusts politicians one favours fixed exchange rates; if one distrusts politicians one favours floating rates.' Discuss.

28. 'Only gold is trusted; therefore the only reliable form of international monetary reform would be a return to the gold standard.' Comment.

29. Why did the gold standard work well in the period before 1914?

30. Compare the 'adjustment problem' of the gold standard in the 1920s with that of the Bretton Woods system in the 1960s.

31. What are reserve currencies? Is the running of a reserve currency an advantage or a disadvantage for Britain?
32. What is meant by an international liquidity problem? How would it be affected by the introduction of floating exchange rates?
33. How have OPEC policies affected the international monetary system?

BIBLIOGRAPHY

Books

J. C. Powicke, D. J. Iles, B. Davies, *Applied Economics*, Edward Arnold, 1972.

B. Tew, *International Monetary Cooperation* 1945–70, Hutchinson, 10th Ed., 1970.

W. M. Scammell, *International Monetary Policy*, Macmillan, 2nd Ed., 1970.

S. J. Wells, *International Economics*, Allen & Unwin, 1969.

M. A. G. van Meerhaeghe, *International Economic Institutions*, Longman, 2nd Ed., 1971.

H. G. Grubel, *The International Monetary System*, Penguin, 1969.

J. M. Livingstone, *Britain and the World Economy*, Penguin, 1966.

L. J. Williams, *Britain and the World Economy* 1919–1970, Fontana, 1971.

V. Anthony, *Britain's Overseas Trade*, Heinemann, 1969.

H. G. Johnson, *The World Economy at the Crossroads*, Oxford, 1965.

W. Arthur Lewis, *Economic Survey* 1919–1939, Allen & Unwin.

R. Triffin, *Gold and the Dollar Crisis*, Yale University Press, 1966.

S. Brittan, *Steering the Economy*, Penguin, 1971.

Sir Roy Harrod, *Reforming the World's Money*, Macmillan, 1966.

S. Brittan, *The Price of Economic Freedom*, Macmillan, 1970.

A. R. Prest and D. J. Coppock, *The UK Economy*, Weidenfeld and Nicholson, 4th Ed., 1972.

Articles

'The World Adjustment Problem', *B.B.R.*, May 1973.

'SDRs and Aid', Lord Kahn, *L.B.R.*, October 1973.

P. Bauer, 'Inflation, SDRs and Aid', *L.B.R.*, July 1973.

R. Triffin, 'The Case for the Demonetization of Gold', *L.B.R.*, January 1974.

P. Bauer, 'The SDR Link Scheme – A Comment', *L.B.R.*, January 1974.

W. B. Reddaway, 'Was $4·86 Inevitable in 1925?', *L.B.R.*, April 1970.

G. Haberler, 'Prospects for the Dollar Standard', *L.B.R.*, July 1972.

'Progress in International Monetary Co-operation', *M.B.R.*, November 1969.

'Currency Crisis – But Not For Sterling', *M.B.R.*, May 1972.

P. M. Oppenheimer, 'What Kind of Mechanism for Reserve Creation?', *W.B.R.*, August 1965.

'Moving Towards International Monetary Reform – Developments since November 1971', *M.B.R.*, November 1972.

'Annual Monetary Survey – No. 19 – Year to April 1968', *M.B.R.*, May 1968.

'Devaluation – For the Record', *M.B.R.*, February 1968.

'Annual Monetary Survey – No. 20 – Year to April 1969', *M.B.R.*, May 1969.

'Annual Monetary Survey – No. 24 – Year to April 1973', *M.B.R.*, May 1973.

'The Retreat from Bretton Woods – The Story So Far', *M.B.R.*, November 1971.

'The Evolution of the Sterling Area – What it Signifies Today', *M.B.R.*, February 1972.

'Some echoes of 1931', *B.B.R.*, February 1968.

'Hot Oil Money', *B.B.R.*, August 1973.

F. Hirsch, 'A fragile freedom', *The Economist*, August 5, 1972.

'What's to become of the IMF?', *The Economist*, May 26, 1973.

'Agreeing to disagree on currencies', *The Economist*, September 9, 1972.

'Crisis in the millpond', *The Economist*, July 14, 1973.

'A pity about the pound', *The Economist*, June 24, 1972.

'Float free and low', *The Economist*, July 1, 1972.

'The pound in a new straitjacket', *The Economist*, April 29, 1972.

'The gold rush', *The Economist*, May 19, 1973.

'The ever-rising yen', *The Economist*, May 6, 1972.

'Monetary reform: how the experts have failed the world', *The Times*, September 9, 1973.

'No time to moan and weep', *The Times*, July 28, 1973.

N. Kaldor, 'Reserves on a commodity standard', *The Times*, September 8, 1971.

'Foundations of world monetary reform', *The Times*, July 27, 1973.

'Seeds of monetary reform could spring from death of gold exchange standard', J. Rueff, *The Times*, December 14, 1973.

Bank of England Quarterly Bulletin, Vol. 12 No 1–4
Vol. 13 No 1–4

Annual and Economic Review I, *The Times*, September 24, 1973.

'Living with floating exchange rates', *The Times*, May 16, 1973.

'Those erratic rates: a foretaste of things to come', *The Economist*, January 22, 1972.

'Thrown to the lions at Nairobi?' *The Economist*, August 25, 1973.

Valery Giscard d'Estaing, 'Banks should be ready to make settlements in gold', *The Times*, Europe Monthly, March 1974.

'Avoiding a recession', *B.B.R.*, February 1974.

D. Kern, 'International Finance and the Euro-dollar market', *N.W.B.R.*, November 1971.

B.B.R. – Barclays Bank Review

L.B.R. – Lloyds Bank Review

M.B.R. – Midland Bank Review

N.W.B.R. – National Westminster Bank Review

W.B.R. – Westminster Bank Review

INDEX

125

STUDIES IN THE BRITISH ECONOMY

THE UNITED KINGDOM AND THE WORLD MONETARY SYSTEM

STUDIES IN THE BRITISH ECONOMY

General Editor: Derek Lee

Core book: The United Kingdom Economy *by the National Institute of Economic and Social Research*